Christ in a Changing World

CHRIST in a
CHANGING
WORLD

Toward an Ethical Christology

Tom F. Driver

CROSSROAD · NEW YORK

8-86

1981
The Crossroad Publishing Company
575 Lexington Avenue, New York, NY 10022

Copyright © 1981 by Tom F. Driver
Printed in the United States of America

Library of Congress Cataloging in Publication Data

Driver, Tom Faw, 1925-
    Christ in a changing world.

    Bibliography: p. 171
    Includes index.
    1. Jesus Christ — Person and offices.   2. Christian
ethics.   I. Title.
BT202.D64   232   81-5552
ISBN 0-8245-0105-5   AACR2

To all who have suffered
at the hands of people
who claimed to act in
the name of Christ,
  this book is dedicated.

Contents

Preface

In August of 1980 at a Christian political rally held in Dallas, Texas, the president of the Southern Baptist Convention, the Reverend Dr. Bailey Smith, declared from the rostrum: "God Almighty does not hear the prayer of a Jew." Questioned later about this statement, the speaker said: "I am pro-Jew. I believe they are God's special people, but without Jesus Christ they are lost. No prayer gets through that is not prayed through Jesus Christ. Jews have an argument with me because they have an argument with the New Testament" (*The New York Times*, September 18, 1980).

The book I offer here was written before Dr. Smith made his inflammatory statement, but it is intended to attack christological ideas that result in thoughts such as he uttered. As a Christian and a teacher of theology, I have a responsibility to examine those presuppositions of Christian doctrine that often lead, in spite of our best intentions, to prejudice and injustice.

This book is not addressed primarily to fundamentalists, who in any case are unlikely to give it a careful reading. It is addressed to liberal Christians, among whom I count myself, insofar as we imagine that the teachings about Christ in the "mainstream" of Christianity are not anti-Semitic, nor racist, nor sexist, nor biased toward the ideologies of the rich at the expense of the poor.

I have come to think that much of what Christianity has to say about Christ is unethical. The fundamentalists do us a great service by exposing, for all to see, certain logical and bigoted results that flow from convictions about Christ regarded as so "fundamental" that even we liberal and modernist Christians do not often challenge them. Whether anyone may do so and continue to be regarded as a Christian is something the reception of this book may clarify.

My previous book *Patterns of Grace* (1977) was an exploration of the decisive role human experience plays in shaping and recognizing the word of God. In its introduction, composed after the rest was done, I said that I had not explored the implications of my perspective for ethics and Christology, which were "matters I hope to take up in a subsequent volume." When I sat down to take them up, I realized how closely intertwined they are. This present book is the result.

What pulls this book "off center" from the most familiar teachings of the churches about Christ is its concern for ethics. Included in human experience, always, are some convictions or assumptions about what is good. Without these we can have no experience of God, Christ, or anything else. Experience is value-laden, and so is Christian doctrine. That is why it will not do to establish our christology first and then figure out its ethical implications. When we do christology we are doing ethics, and when we do ethics we are doing something or other with Christ, whose ethical impact on the world, for better or worse, not even an atheist may plausibly deny.

As I explain in the following pages, what we Christians have some control over is what we shall teach. This book concerns itself with what we shall *ethically* teach about Christ. To raise this question in light of present-day experience is to plunge into the most basic questions concerning God, life, and the future of humanity. It is to dive into waters over one's head. I make no claim to examine these matters as deeply as they ought to be examined. Leaping into waters too deep for me, I call now for help. I have little doubt that a number of rescuers will be glad to pull me back to the nether shore, but I want to know if there is a shore on the other side. Are there those who can help me reach it? At the least, does anyone think I have dived in the right direction?

I am not the first to have dived in this direction. Some before me are named in the pages hereafter. Let others also be named. I am mindful, too, of those whose names are lost to history and who yearned for a Christ surpassing the one who had been preached to them or who was to be found in the pages of scripture.

I have a host of living persons to thank, but I shall name only those who read or heard my text and told me how to improve it:

Anne Barstow, Shirley Cloyes, Newton Dougherty, Carolyn Heil-brun, Carter Heyward, the Theological Colloquium, and the members of my seminar ST 470 at Union Theological Seminary in New York, the New Haven Theological Discussion Group, and the students and faculty at Queens Theological College in Ontario. These kind people encouraged me to see that my secret thoughts about Jesus Christ were on *their* minds, too, whether or not they agreed with my conclusions. Special thanks are owed to my careful editor at Crossroad, Justus George Lawler. I am indebted to Bobby Alexander for certain of the ideas in Chapter 8.

Anne Barstow, who is my wife, gave me the response to my text which was at once the most exhilarating and the saddest of all. She said, "You are speaking of Jesus in the way I wish I had heard when I was young. You are making him alive for me. But it has come too late to prevent me from feeling shut out from a full relationship with Christ." This from a woman who has not left the church and who continues to suffer within it.

The text to follow has only one footnote. I have adopted what is called "the author-date method" of citing my sources and refer-ences. Author and date of a relevant text are given in parentheses, with notation of pages when called for. At the end of the book is a Reference List, alphabetical and chronological by author, which the reader may use to identify the books and articles to which I refer. When the source is ancient, or is a modern work translated from a foreign language, the author-date method presents some problems. In most of these cases, the date given is the date of com-position or first publication, the better to clue the reader to the time of the work's origin. The Reference List gives also the date of all editions and translations actually quoted. In all cases where I have not found the date of composition or first publication, I cite merely the date of the edition I have used.

It is my desire that the reasonings put forward in the following pages may contribute to a convergence between ethical conscience and christic expectation in this day and time.

TOM F. DRIVER

Union Theological Seminary
New York

Christ in a Changing World

·1·

Introduction

Persons I meet socially and students in the classroom ask me the same question: "What is theology?" The students have already enrolled themselves in a theological seminary, but still they ask; and full-fledged theologians often ask it of each other. It seems the right question with which to begin a theological book, and I shall quickly answer.

I take theology itself to be the answer to a question, or at least the attempt to answer. That question is: What should the church teach about God? In practice, the word "theology" refers broadly to the church's teaching about any subject whatever. In the strict sense, it refers to what the church, given its history and mission, *should* teach.

When I offer this definition to students, some of them retort: "That's not theology, that's dogma." Ours is an independent, inter-denominational seminary to which many have come in order to get away from dogmatism. They want from their teachers a more philosophical definition of theology, one that will refer to science or the arts or psychology or social justice or whatever they are most interested in. They don't find reference to the church very helpful.

A long explanation of why theology is tied to the church would take us into the sociology of knowledge. Briefly, the point is that every intellectual discipline has a social base. Ideas do not really have "a life of their own." They have the life of the social group that is interested in them and finds them useful. We do not well understand a science, an art, a psychology, or a social theory until we know whose interests it serves, and why and how. The idea of a "pure" science is close to being a pure fiction. Certainly there is no theology that is "pure" of the vested interests of religious communities and their desire, from good motives or bad, to perpetuate their convictions.

I use the word "theology" to refer to Christian theology, although it should be clear there are other kinds. Each kind, Jewish, Islamic, Buddhist, Hindu, etc., has a social base in a religious community and addresses itself to the teaching that is pertinent to it. The concerns of every theology that is not hopelessly parochial extend far beyond religion — into philosophy, politics, economics, law, medicine, and more — but the base is always an existing religious community. When this is lost sight of, either by the theologian or the reader, theology starts to float in the clouds. Then people ask, "What is theology?" and I try to return them to the base, which in the case of Christianity is the church existing in the world. If I write now a book that has no bearing upon what the church teaches, it will not be a book of theology.

To be more accurate, we should speak of Christian churches, in the plural, and of many Christian theologies. Alexis de Tocqueville, that early observer of life in America, being particularly struck by religious pluralism in this land, said that here "every man's hat is his Church." Armchair theologians like me have to be careful not to address ourselves to some ideal, imaginary church existing only in our heads. It helps me, and my reader too, I hope, to know that my identification is Protestant, my denomination Methodist, and my teaching is done in an ecumenical school. I belong to a recognizable breed, and whatever I say to the churches at large comes from that perspective.

It was courageous of Karl Barth to call his theology a *Church Dogmatics* (1936-1969). It showed that he was not afraid to say what is the base and purpose of Christian theology. The base is the church, and the purpose is to help it define what to teach. I think most of the content of Barth's answer to the question was extremely wrongheaded, but he did have the right question.

"Dogma" is simply the ancient Greek word for what one teaches. Since the Enlightenment, the connotation of the word has become pejorative. We use it to refer to the opinions of people we don't agree with, especially if we think their opinions are not very rational. Still, we live, as the Greeks did, in a society of many competing dogmas, and this is probably more true since the Enlightenment than before. Education, we have discovered, does not get rid of dogmas; it multiplies them. In this situation, the churches do not find it easy to know what to teach and what not to teach. That accounts for the so-called crisis in theology today.

What should the churches in North America these days be saying and doing? I write this book out of concern for that question. I do not share a widespread assumption that the churches are irrelevant. On the contrary, I am upset by how very much relevance they do have and how wrongly it is directed. As I see it, the United States is not a secular nation but a reactionary religious one. The media exude theology night and day. I do not mean only some implicit theologies one can detect in secular TV, film, and publishing. I mean explicit religious teaching all over this land. The churches and quasi-independent evangelists are teaching up a storm, and people are getting the messages. The results, for the most part, are very unethical. They amount to what Dorothee Sölle has called "christofascism." Much of the churches' treaching about Christ has turned into something that is dictatorial in its heart and is preparing society for an American fascism. Most people do not notice, because they think it is enough to call upon the name of Jesus. It is not enough, as Jesus himself said; it never has been, and it has always been dangerous.

What then *should* the churches teach about Christ? As the word "theology" means teaching about God, so christology, the subject of this book, means teaching about Christ. What should it mean to call Jesus the Christ? What is the relation between Christ and God, and how are they both related to North Americans today? What has Christ to do with people who are not and never will be Christians? What has Christ got to do with the dangerous problems of the twentieth century—war, atomic energy, overpopulation, decay of the environment, mass starvation, and the systematic oppression of poor people?

We live on a sick planet. The earth is sick with suffering, and we who dwell here are like the inhabitants of a city struck by a plague. In such a time, what, if anything, should the church teach about

Christ? Is Jesus our savior now, or has he also caught the contagion? What has the church to say to a world on the verge of collapse?

I am going to write, then, a theological tract, although I hope it will not be simplistic. I intend it to be a christology worked out in the context of socioethical concern. I shall dogmatically oppose any separation between christology and ethics or between ethics and social justice. The book would not be worth writing if theology alone were in crisis. Our crisis is social. It seems to me that's what the Bible said it was all along, and I am angry that the Bible's religious passion for social justice has been turned into a teaching about individual salvation, which has the net effect of rationalizing and perpetuating social iniquity.

I come to the writing of this work on the heels of a previous book, *Patterns of Grace: Human Experience as Word of God* (1977). When the book was finished, I realized that what it had to say about God was not matched by sufficient attention to the doctrine of Christ. I would need to think that through. I realized also that the emphasis I had placed on one's own experiences, becoming aware of them and taking responsibility for them, had overshadowed an idea which is in fact very important to me: that human experience is social through and through. Then it occurred to me that the social dimension of human experience and the christic dimension of religion belong together. Not that one causes the other, but that the sociality of Christ is what we should be seeing and teaching. To know what to say about Christ, we have to know where we stand in relation to the whole human race, for that relation is what Christ is about.

For all its individualism, *Patterns of Grace* is about participation. It insists that we collaborate with our physical and social environment to form the "world" in which we make our decisions. It insists that God is not outside that process but within it in the same sense as we. It declares that God does nothing all alone, *is* nothing all alone, and acts in collaboration with us to co-create whatever is made. It therefore involves God in human history and sees God as one who changes in the course of time. Openness to change is necessary for the awareness of experience, from which alone we derive the motive and the means to alleviate oppression. It can be noticed that oppressors, if they have to justify what they are doing, usually make appeal to some divinity or some principle beyond the reach of experience. They prefer to blot out the experiences of suffering they themselves inflict and which threaten to undermine their power. But the sufferers know something given them in their flesh, therefore more certain than any principle: their pain, and their desire for it to cease. Pain is the beginning of knowledge. Blotting it out of consciousness is the maintenance of ignorance.

The participation of God in human pain, which the New Testament dramatizes as the passion of Jesus, means that God undergoes change. That is what it meant for Jesus, and I shall argue that the risen Christ also changes in time.

The christology proposed in this book is radical. Although there will be some who think it not christology at all, certainly not orthodox, perhaps not Christian, it is not my intention to desert the Christian faith, abandon my love of Jesus, or cease looking for Christ to come. On the contrary, I am persuaded, to paraphrase St. Paul, that not even the doubts of modernity nor the depths of our iconoclasm can separate us from the love of God in Christ (cf. Rom. 8:38–39). If I am concerned that the worship of God in Christ not divide Christian from Jew, man from woman, clergy from laity, white from black, or rich from poor, I see in this no betrayal of God's creative word. If I warn us Christians of the danger of idolatry in regarding Christ Jesus as a past perfection, I do not believe I have forsaken that Jesus who nourished me in my youth and still evokes both my ardor and my irritation. Indeed, it is my very love of Jesus that prompts me not to give over to him the whole of my conscience, judgment, and faith. If we are empty before him and have no identity of our own, we do not love. Love is a kind of dialogue, which is not possible if the Christ of the past contains all that we need to know. These thoughts lead me to a firm belief in the resurrection of Christ Jesus, which I interpret not merely as a myth or a symbol but as a true historical event.

"If Christ be not raised," St. Paul wrote, "your faith is vain" (I Cor. 15:17). The sentence is perhaps as close as any to a classic christological text. I cite it in agreement not because it has classical authority, but because it so well expresses the heart of a christology oriented to the present-future. The issue is not whether there has ever been a Christ, which would be a topic in the history of religions. The issue is whether Christ lives today with liberating power for our future. This is the existential meaning of the resurrection of Jesus, and without it the word "Christ" would be out of place.

It is of course possible to take the word "Christ" as a symbol expressive of an archetype in the unconscious mind and thus to treat Christian faith in the manner of Carl Jung, sweeping aside all concern with a historical resurrection (see Homans 1979). This is a modern version of an ancient thought: to suppose that Christ, as the subject of Christian faith, is an object of internal (and eternal) soul, having no connection, or at most an accidental one, with the external world. Christ then floats free of history, so to speak, and so do God and the soul. This neo-Platonic idea has colored a large part of the church's thinking since the third century. Its resurgence today presents the church with a very clear-cut decision to be made about its teaching. As we have a residual neo-Platonism on the one hand, which would, along with much popular Jesus-piety, internalize Christ and turn religious teaching away from the socioethical world, on the other hand we have a modern historical sensibility, coming to us from the Enlightenment and from the nineteenth century, which beckons us to understand God and ourselves fundamentally as agents of historical development. We are apparently asked to choose between the eternal soul and the historical world. Of course, we would like to have it both ways, but the split in our culture and in the churches is too deep for that to be possible immediately. We are still faced with one of the oldest tensions within Christianity, reflected in the New Testament itself: whether Christ was and is an active agent in the real world or only the subject of an internal process called "faith."

This tension accounts for the theological importance of the historical resurrection of Jesus. Paul's words make it clear that he knew some Christians were ready to separate faith in Christ from Jesus' resurrection, which would turn faith inward or skyward, disconnecting it from the direct action of God in history. "If Christ was not raised, your faith has nothing in it" (I Cor. 15:17, NEB). Is this a rational claim in light of modern historical thinking? Can we believe it without becoming superstitious and thus falling back into that same internalization of faith we are trying to avoid?

What we need is to keep our rationality while letting go of that rational*ism* which views "history" as a realm of proofs. I am thinking of proof in two senses. First, historical research cannot "prove" or "disprove" the resurrection of Jesus. All it can do is assemble data and conjectures about the composition of the stories. The historicality of the event, like that of anything else that has ever happened, is a matter of judgment so complex that it can never be finally settled. As Ernst Troeltsch pointed out long ago, historical conclusions are judgments not of certainty but of probability (see Harvey 1966, p. 17). It takes no seer to demonstrate that Jesus' resurrection was and is highly improbable: that is the whole point of its importance. Intellectual honesty on this matter requires of Christians an uneasy conscience, lest they exploit for the sake of credulity a loophole in the logic of historical science. But this again is the point: resurrection faith requires, as part of its meaning, an uneasy historical conscience, and this not only about the resurrection of Jesus but about much other history as well. Those who are sure that they know what has happened in history, and what did not happen, are a menace to the kingdom of God. They can be found among "true believing" Christians as well as among secularists and atheists. The former insist upon the resurrection of Jesus as a historical "fact" rather than a historical judgment made in the risk of faith. One of the risks of Christian faith is that one may be wrong about history. In these matters, contrary to what Paul Tillich said, faith provides no "guarantee" (Tillich 1957, pp. 113f.). Faith cannot escape the relativity of history and of historical judgment. On the contrary, it is called *to* them. Relativity carries in its fragile basket the moral meaning of human and divine life.

Second, the historical resurrection of Jesus, even if we hold that it did occur, "proves" nothing about the truth of Christian faith. The mere fact of Jesus' appearance to his disciples after he had been dead and buried does not make him the Christ nor prove that anyone should have faith in him. The meaning of the resurrection, like that of any other historical event, does not lie in the sheer fact that it happened. One has always to ask, so what? Does it make any difference to us now? If it does not, then we have no interest in the matter. A maxim I propounded in *Patterns of Grace* (1977, p. 41) is pertinent here: "That which makes no difference cannot be known." Christological method must concern itself not only with the resurrection of Jesus once upon a time but with the difference that event makes now in our present-future.

Nowhere in Christian faith does the coincidence of subjectivity and objectivity become clearer or more decisive than where the resurrection of Jesus is pondered. One means to speak of the resurrection as a quite real, "objective," fact of history, as objective, let us say, as the slaughter of Jews in Hitler's Germany, and one can do so only with great subjective risk and passion. To do otherwise, as is also true of the Holocaust, is to falsify the very object of which one speaks. The scientific method of historical research, as practiced today, encourages a dispassionate evaluation of data. Christological method concerning resurrection encourages the deepest passion. This reveals an antagonism between faith and historical method but not, I think, between faith and history. The coincidence of subjectivity and objectivity which the resurrection highlights shows how crucial is historical reality in Christian meaning. In the final analysis, Christianity is a view of life which has all the intensity and the keen observation of a powerful work of art. Faith and art are alike in that, for both, the objective and the subjective fuse. It makes, then, much difference whether this is regarded as Christianity's flight from history into aesthetics or whether it is a justified raising of history into a godly subject. Those who doubt that it may be the latter should turn their gaze not upon the past but upon the destitution of hopeless masses of people in our own period of history. Whoever is not moved by this plight to passionate historical subjectivity will not be able to understand a resurrection christology.

Most church architecture, liturgy, vocabulary, and theological expression conspire in the illusion that Christianity is primarily oriented to the past. Insofar as this is not an illusion but the actual state of Christianity, it may be regarded as a falling away from resurrection faith. It also shows a profound misapprehension of the movement of time in human life. For a creature with consciousness and moral responsibility, time does not flow from the past into the present on its way to the future. Neither does it go the opposite way, from the future into the past by way of the present. Its movement is more complicated. Truth to tell, it is the movement of a moral agent that is complicated, and this requires a complex view of the connections between the present, the future, and the past.

Aristotle had said somewhere that time is the measure of motion. Augustine (*Confessions,* Book XI) answered that it is better to say that time is the measure of purpose. Unlike Aristotle, he was interested in how a moral consciousness experiences time, and he rightly saw that it has to do with one's sense of purpose at any given moment. Although what I say hereafter differs somewhat from Augustine, he is nonetheless a great help to anyone who wants to think about time. To use him as an occasion for reflection is a good example of what I shall advocate in general terms below.

A purpose, which I prefer to call an "intention," is something that is alive. It therefore exists in the present and can be experienced only by being presently active, like hunger and thirst. Otherwise, it is not an intention but only the memory of one or perhaps the dream of having one later. However, as Jean-Paul Sartre has pointed out, there are no memories or dreams without present intentions (Sartre 1948). Purposeful time (and we may reasonably doubt whether there is any other kind, especially if time originates with a purposeful God) is therefore present time oriented toward the future. I cannot intend to do something yesterday. I can only intend toward the future. Only by knowing myself as presently tending to go forward in time can I have any purpose whatever. For this reason it makes sense to regard human time as present-future time, to which the concepts of past-present and past-future are ancillary.

Imagine that time does not move in a straight line but in a loop (cf. Driver 1977, pp. 124–128, and *passim*). The line starts in the present with an intention regarding the future: to start something, to complete something, to change something, whatever. On its way into the future, the intended action and the attempt to envision it encounter the unknown. How can I imagine what has not yet happened, let alone any problems ahead? This question (or its unconscious equivalent) evokes memory. I have no clue to the future except such as may be provided by knowledge of the past in conjunction with present intention. This causes the line of time to form a loop. Present-future purpose loops backward into memory, looking for data to inform the present-future course of action. Not everything it finds is relevant or suitable. Bringing what it chooses as relevant, the line returns to the present, where evaluation and judgment reside. A decision is made. The intention, modified by recollection, goes forward into the future as action.

The loop of time into the past is so often made by sheer reflex that we do not notice how it works. Every second of our lives we are summoning up memories to inform our flow of actions. Many of these "memories" are encoded in neural reflexes, the better to have them work by semiautomation so that we do not have to think about them. The fully unconscious actions, such as digesting food in the stomach or producing antibodies in the system, were learned long ago by our genetic ancestors, and only much scientific study has revealed how we do them.

Moral freedom requires that the loop of time from present-future into past and back again to present-future rise above being a mere reflex and become reflective. This has been made possible in human beings by the evolution of a large cerebral cortex. Under it lie two older brains still in use: the "reptilian brain" working mostly by reflex, and the "middle brain" which houses a great deal of memory that can on occasion become conscious. The job of the cerebral cortex is to summon up stored memories, make sense of them, and bring this sense to bear upon our actions. There seems to be a more rational, linguistic way of doing this, associated with one hemisphere in the brain, and a more intuitive, nonverbal way associated with the other. Even the less verbal hemisphere, however, is not unreflective.

Insofar as our relation to the past is moral, it is reflective. Human life loses its moral quality when it is content with a reflexive use of the past. In everyday terms, this means repeating or perpetuating a course of action simply because it existed in the past. To be tradition-bound is to want to reflect (mirror) the past without critical reflection. Sometimes this posture results from sheer failure of imagination. More often it is a strategy for maintaining the power of an elite. Occasionally it is a necessary mechanism of survival, just as one's biological reflexes are designed to protect the organism by doing automatically what worked before. Indeed, there is a genuine motive of survival in all honoring of tradition. When a society or an institution, however, makes survival its main purpose and therefore tradition its main value, it begins to become immoral. When a church does so, it pulls away from resurrection faith, turning instead to a reflexive use of the past and an idolatry of memory. This is so even if the memory is of Jesus Christ.

The main purpose of the church is not to remember Jesus. Its main purpose, surely, is to participate now, in present-future time, in the redemption of the world. To this end have the life, death, and resurrection of Jesus in past time been given. It is for christology and the churches to make a reflective, not a reflexive, use of that gift. If we move in the freedom whereby the risen Christ is making us free, our continuity with Christ past will take care of itself. It is in any case not a continuity of letter but of spirit, and the right form of it will be revealed in the education of conscience by the sufferings of the present age. Such at least is the confidence I have that Christ is not dead and is therefore free to approach us in a form we cannot foretell.

·2·

Method for an Ethical Christology

Christology is the answer, or an attempt to answer, what the churches should teach about Christ. If my answer is to be taken with any seriousness, I am supposed to say how I propose to go about finding it. This is called theological or, in the present case, christological method. I think a person who sets out to tell the churches what to think and say is a little bit crazy. I am therefore reminded of what Polonius said about Hamlet, who was driven to frenzy by the immorality of the royal court at Elsinore: "Though this be madness, yet there is method in't" (*Hamlet*, II. ii. 205). Exasperated by certain kinds of fidelity to Christ which murder everything Jesus was about, I need a method to redeem my madness.

Since the church is the social base of theology, a possible method of ascertaining what it should teach is to assemble its people and ask them. If there were agreement on the right questions, a poll might be taken by mail, but there is not. The time-honored procedure is to convene a number of delegates to debate in council, which is how the Nicene and other historic creeds came to be. The process goes on today in denominational and ecumenical assemblies which formulate church teaching on controversial issues such as homosexuality, abortion, revolution, racism, sexism, and so on.

In principle, both Protestantism and Catholicism recognize the church itself as the author of theology. In practice, theological writing has become a specialty which most people, including many church leaders, do not pretend to understand. The result is a tendency in church councils to separate unavoidable ethical issues of the kind mentioned above from the more arcane topics that appear to be strictly theological. A clear example has occurred while I write these pages.

The press has announced that the Episcopal convention in 1980 will receive a committee report encouraging diocesan bishops to permit the ordination of avowed homosexuals. Although this proposal amounts to a major change in church policy, the report does not seem to consider any corresponding change in church teaching about God or Christ. Interviewed on the radio, the bishop who chaired the committee avoids discussion of God, Christ, and sin, even though the interviewer, with the common sense of a good reporter, tries to pursue these topics.

The churches like to leave basic theological tenets alone while focusing upon specific moral issues. To do so makes a certain conservative sense from a sociological point of view, but it confuses everyone. If God is the same yesterday and today, and if our teaching about God does not change, how can our ethics change? The inconsistency is readily apparent, and the more liberal churches are weakened by it. The fundamentalist-evangelical churches have the advantage of consistency. They maintain that God and the teaching about Him (*sic*) do *not* change, and neither does Christian morality. "Old time religion," seeking to avoid the complexities of change, has a strong appeal. I see North American Christianity strung out between two poles: on the one hand, a liberalism devoted to social change while lacking a clear theology of change in God; on the other, a conservativism resisting change and thus allied with reactionary political forces. The large historic denominations such as Baptist, Methodist, Episcopal, and Roman Catholic are split down the middle, their right hands at war with their left.

For better or worse, theology will go as the churches go. By daily practice as well as by official pronouncements, the churches do teach, and their theologies do evolve. Few individual theologians affect this process very greatly at the present time.

Nevertheless, an important function belongs to theologians like myself who have one foot in the church, the other outside, and who

may write whatever we please because we are not speaking officially. Our task is to influence the churches by saying things that may
catch the attention and prod the intellectual conscience of persons
in the church who do determine its direction. Such persons are in
the pews as well as in pulpits and high office. Some have a seminary
education and some do not. One must write as clearly as possible.
But how does one decide what to say? What method am I to use to
determine what the church ought to teach about Christ?

Most discussions of theological method begin with the past, or
else with what Paul Tillich called "the eternal truth" of the
Christian message (Tillich 1951, p. 3). The assumption is that the
Christian community has been founded upon the life, death, and
resurrection of Jesus some two thousand years ago. This decisive
event in the past is seen to have been recorded in the New Testament, anticipated in the Old, and interpreted from one generation
to the next in the history of theology. There are thus two principal
guides to theological thinking: scripture and tradition. In the sixteenth century, Protestants and Catholics fought bitterly over which
of these was primary, Martin Luther having set out to reform the
church by appealing to scripture in order to purge tradition of its
errors and abuses. Today there is not much argument about scripture versus tradition between Catholic and Protestant theologians,
so much have they learned from each other in the last few decades.
The consensus seems to be that scripture occupies a uniquely
authoritative place within tradition.

If one starts with the past, granting primary authority to what
may be called the "scriptural tradition," the theological task becomes that of interpreting a legacy, and this in such way as to high-
light its relevance in the present. This may be done, for example, in
a Barthian fashion by stressing the alien, unexpected, incompre-
hensible demand which the revelation in Christ makes upon sinful
humanity. The gospel is seen as undercutting all assumptions of
culture. By contrast, one can adopt a Tillichian method and set out
to show a fundamental correlation between human need and the
saving truth in Christ. In either case, as in most christologies, the
initial assumption is that Christ is a gift humanity has received from
God in past history. Christological formulations become a set of in-
structions accompanying the gift. We are told how to interpret a

Christ who has arrived in the wrappings of scriptural, creedal, and liturgical tradition. A Barth will tell us to begin with the part labeled Word of God, however strange it appears, and go on from there, carefully discarding all shreds of human experience that have unfortunately attached themselves to the Word during transit. A Tillich will advise us to arrange everything according to Being, in which case Christ will appear as New Being, the very truth for which we have, perhaps unconsciously, been looking. Virtually every modern liberal theologian will tell us to place Christ at "the center of history," wherever that is. Revolutionary theologians supply a label to be affixed saying "Liberator," while conservatives provide one reading "My Lord and Savior."

Amid such clamor a sentence from Robert Pirsig's *Zen and the Art of Motorcycle Maintenance* comes to mind. The instruction sheet in the cardboard carton said: "Assembly of Japanese bicycle require great peace of mind" (Pirsig 1975, p. 158).

Life does not start with prepackaged materials. It does not start in the past, and neither does good teaching about Christ. The primary question we have to ask is not who Jesus was, nor who the disciples thought he was, nor what his early followers had in mind when they called him Christ. I shall consider those questions in due time, for they have a certain importance, but they are not fundamental. The decisive questions are who Jesus is today, what *we* have in mind if we call him Christ, and what business we intend shall go on between him and us and the world. The answer is not entirely in our hands, but then it is not entirely in Christ's hands, either.

We do not, in the method I propose, start by figuring out who Jesus was or is and then decide what our relation to him ought to be. We start with the existing relation, which we can discern in our behavior and our expectations of the future. All we can ever know about Jesus and any other persons is how they affect us in relation, what they stimulate us to desire or to avoid, and what they lead us to expect henceforth. Relation, manifest in behavior, is prior to identity.

"In the beginning," said Martin Buber, "is the relation" (Buber 1923, p. 69). The pedestal upon which theology has so often put Jesus isolates him and corrodes his relation to us. It tends toward the christofascism of which Dorothee Sölle has spoken (above, p. 3). It does not express *my* relation to Jesus nor that of Christians who appear to me most ethically sensitive, and so I propose not to start from the top or the foot of any pedestal.

What matters is the behavior of the church today and tomorrow. We do not have to call the church into existence; it is already here. The ethical question is not, "How did it get here?" but, "What next?" I believe that we have fallen into an un-Christian trap of regarding Jesus as the founder of the church and Christ as the foundation of the whole world, with the consequent result that too many have lost their relation to him as friend, helper, and prophet. We try to *re*cover the authentic Christ of the beginning, failing thereby to *dis*cover the friend of the present and future. Our theology is too often a kind of nostalgia, devoted primarily to memory and reconstruction. In such manner do we interpret the New Testament testimony to Christ crucified, neglecting the obvious fact that the writers of the New Testament were speaking of something that was for them startlingly *new*. They were writing *contemporary* history in the course of their teaching about Jesus, and I propose that we do the same, not in order to imitate them but because the present-future is the locus of life in a way that the past can never be, not even the godly past recorded in scripture. I think Jesus in his own day had a similar attitude to life, spirit, and scriptural tradition; but I would feel compelled to say these things even if he did not. The Jesus we know from scripture, insofar as scripture is ancient, is not the decisive authority for teaching about Jesus. If we say that he is, we restrict categorically the freedom of God to "make all things new."

God is not eternally the same. We need to understand this in order to appreciate the religious and ethical value of our experience, which is another way of saying our history. The active relation of God to humanity, which the Old and New Testaments both emphasize, can only mean that God is party to at least some historical changes. Whatever God's transcendence of history may mean in the Bible, it does not mean immutability nor eternal sameness. A similar point must now be made with regard to Christ.

"What's done," said Lady Macbeth, "is done" (*Macbeth*, III. ii. 12). Her words convey an apparently commonsensical understanding of the past: Whatever it was it was, and it will never be anything else. However obvious such a thought may seem, it is neither an ethical nor a Christian view of the past. Lady Macbeth's aphorism was phrased to smother her husband's conscience after he, with her help, had planned the murder of King Banquo in his sleep in their house. By saying that the past is past, she rationalizes her desire not to repent, not to change course in the present. Whenever and wherever the past is regarded either as fixed or as decisively authoritative, one may perceive an intention to persist in a present course of action, or at least to appear to do so.

The eruption of Jesus into the life of Palestine twenty centuries ago proved to be a radical event because it so drastically upset the past. Contrary to the Herodian puppet government under the sway of Rome, unlike the priesthood which ran the Temple and the civil-religious court (the Sanhedrin), and in conflict with Pharisaic piety, Jesus refused to interpret the scriptural tradition of Israel as fixed, final, or clearly normative. In his teaching, the past was not something already done, to be described in the perfect tense and adhered to as perfectly as possible, but something still alive, active, and changing. So taken, it was to prepare for a new kind of life, which Jesus called the "kingdom of God." The living God was not to be seen as the Lord of a completed, therefore dead, past. "God is not the God of the dead, but of the living" (Matt. 22:32). Since Jesus prefaced this statement by quoting Exodus 3:6, "I am . . . the God of Abraham, the God of Isaac, and the God of Jacob," it followed that in his mind these ancestors were not dead, or did not have to remain so even if they had been buried. The thought was echoed later in the Apostles' Creed, which says that "Jesus Christ our Lord" shall return "to judge the quick and the dead." If the dead are still awaiting judgment, their story is not over, and they are not beyond the touch of life.

That the living power of God controverted the finality of death was the most radical note struck by early Christianity. It ran athwart the teachings of Jewish religion (for the most part), Greek and Roman religion, and popular naturalism. It scandalized some because it flew in the face of common sense, others because it did not refer to an inherent immortality of the soul but to the miraculous power of God, others because it was linked with faith in

Yahweh instead of one or more of the dying and rising gods then widely worshipped; and it offended still others because it was linked with the claim that Jesus had been resurrected.

To deny the finality of death is also to deny the authority assumed to belong to government, law, tradition, religious observance, natural causation, and anything else that may be regarded as "the way it is." If death is not final, all the cards in the deck may be wild. Religious and political authorities rightly saw in such a belief an anarchistic impulse, which they did everything they could to exterminate.

It was not long, however, before the anarchistic impulse unleashed by the preaching of the resurrection appeared threatening to the church itself. This happened as soon as the scattered Christian communities, which sprang up in many places, faced the twin concerns of their survival and their mode of relation to each other. This was already happening as the New Testament was being written. Its occurrence marks the beginning of what we know as "church," for it initiates the recognizable institutional character of the Christian religion. By the same token, it marks the beginning of Christian theology, which arises when the teaching of Christians becomes problematic. Christology begins here, too, and in a way which makes our theological task today very difficult.

In order to preserve and unify itself, the early church turned the teaching of Jesus inside out. The same Jesus who had taught that nothing is final except the kingdom of God in the present-future, was proclaimed to have been the final form of God. He became not only "the Word of God" but God's *last* word. By this masterstroke of transformation, whereby the most open became the most closed, Christianity cut itself off from Judaism and eventually became the cultural religion of Rome, Europe, and America. That something is very wrong with it has not become readily apparent until the twentieth century. Two facts of our time are driving many in the Christian camp to cry out against our own christological tradition. The first is the decline of the political and the moral stature of Euro-American culture.

As Western culture goes ever deeper into crisis in our century, students of religion are quick to note that part of the problem is christological. Some writers, such as T. S. Eliot, Christopher Daw-

son, Malcolm Muggeridge, and the many propagandists of funda-
mentalism, advocate a return to "high christology," since that had
been the centerpiece of Euro-American culture in the days of its
hegemony. They diagnose the social problem as secularism, the culture's loss of its Christian foundation. They would restore Christ to
his throne. Others, myself included, will not advocate a return to
the "good old days," for we think this neither possible nor ethical.
We fear christofascism, which we see as the political direction of all
attempts to place Christ at the center of social life and history. Nor
do we think that Christ should be at the center of one's personal life
if not at the center of society. We therefore think that we must have
a new kind of christology or none at all. We do not want the church
to be teaching that Christ is the center of the world while the world
is crumbling, nor while the poor people in the world, who are the
vast majority of its population, are far from the centers of public
power. We would stress the identification of Jesus with the poor and
the destitute, thereby finding it impossible also to identify him, as
past ages did, with offices of privilege.

We do not seek, then, a "high" christology, and by the same
token we do not seek a "low" one. We seek a christology having little
or nothing to do with the vertical imagery of high and low, while
having much to do with the lateral movement of history and the
time tracks of experience. We would see Jesus as our companion,
not our goal, for we see ourselves as a wilderness people having now
to cross a terrain of perilous canyons in which it is possible to lose
all — our souls, our bodies, our world, and our God.

The other fact of our time evoking Christian protest against
christological tradition is the slaughter of the European Jews in the
Holocaust, for which, as many eyes discern, christology has been
deeply responsible. Christian anti-Semitism stems from christological decisions made in the first century. When Christians came to
regard Christ as the final word of God, on whom alone salvation depended, they had no choice but to regard most Jews as having
"refused" their savior. These Jews were viewed like relatives who
would not come to a family reunion. Therefore they were seen as
worse than the Gentiles, who did not belong to the family except by
adoption. In this attitude, stemming directly from christology, lay
the germ of a more severe thought which was later to bear violent

fruit in persecutions and slaughters: Jews were not really persons. Human rights (the rights of full citizens) did not belong to them except by the charity of the Christian state. It would be better if Jews did not exist, since they were by definition the "refusers" (and the killers) of Christ. On this terrible subject few have written with more clarity than Rosemary Ruether in *Faith and Fratricide* (1974), a book every Christian should read.

A latent doctrine of nonpersons has been the plague of Christianity throughout its history. I do not deny that Christianity has also fostered an opposite doctrine leading to the regard of all souls as sacred, therefore entitled politically to democratic rights. However, the latent doctrine of nonpersons has a special affinity with christology, particularly the so-called high christologies that stress the priesthood and kingship of the Son of God, and the evangelical ones that proclaim Jesus as the one and only "Lord and Savior." The dangerous factor here is the compound of universalism and exclusivism. If there is one, and one only, way to salvation, and if this "way" has the revealed form of Jesus, what rights have those who "refuse" the way or do not correspond to the form?

The latent doctrine of nonpersons showed itself first as anti-Semitism, which was voiced in the New Testament in the Fourth Gospel and in certain phrasings to which the apostle Paul seems to have felt himself driven. It spilled over, however, into what we recognize today as racism and sexism. Women and persons of color were surely among those who followed the "way" of Christ, but they were not seen as corresponding to the form of Jesus. In Europe at least, and in North America up until a decade ago, it did not occur to any white person that Jesus was not white. Certainly he was not female. Nonmales and nonwhites therefore were in peril of being regarded as nonpersons by virtue of their generic difference from the Son of God. I am not suggesting that Christianity was the major cause of racism and sexism, only that it was easily invaded by them and added powerful rationalizations to them because of the way it had chosen to regard Christ and because of its history of anti-Semitism, in which the latent doctrine of the nonperson had first come into Christian thinking.

The attitude and behavior of Christians toward Jews are crucial in the ethical history of the church. I mean not only past history but also, and more importantly for us, present and future history. As the ethical quality of Jesus is manifest most clearly in his relation to persons not of his kind (women, foreigners, social outcasts), so the ethical value of the churches today can be judged by their relation to persons and groups who are not of their following. Among these, the Jewish people provide, as they so often have done in history, a special indicator. As St. Paul, himself a Jew, recognized, the Jews seem to be a thorn put into Christian flesh by God. What Paul did not say, and what must now be said by Christian hindsight, is that Christians have put swords, hammers, bullets, and gas into Jewish flesh and may not claim God as their authority for doing it. For this reason, and because Christianity needs to recover the ethical sensitivity which the Jewish conscience has carried better than the Christian, the churches' teaching about Christ must come under judgment and find a new character, lest it lead to some new holocaust in the future.

The main features of the method I propose to follow are anticipated in what I have already said. It will be helpful to enumerate them and provide brief commentary.

First, the proposed christology shall be subjected, while it is formulated, to ethical judgment. The procedure is not to develop a christology first and inquire into its ethical consequences later, as if there were some hope that we could first see the truth concerning Christ and later deduce a right ethic from it. No perception and no concept arises in the human mind apart from the thinking subject's intentionality toward its neighbor and its world (Driver 1977; Sartre 1948 and 1962). Whatever word or truth or challenge of faith Jesus gives is given to us as moral agents. Conscience is the initial character of human life, a point made very clearly in the biblical story of creation and fall, which is entirely concerned with right relations among God, the world, and human beings. We may question whether the relations as depicted in Genesis 1–2 are adequate to our conscience today (for example, the man-woman relation between Adam and Eve and the child-father relation between humanity and God), but we cannot doubt that the story is predicated upon conscience, beginning with that of God, who "decides" that there should be a world and that the one created is "good." Before we trust any theological doctrine we should ask what is its socioethical consequence. There are Marxists and others who believe that this criterion invalidates all theology. I do not agree, but I readily accept the burden of proof. The church should teach nothing about God or Jesus which does not make positive contribution to social justice. In my opinion, this means that the church's christology should be as radical in our time as was the life of Jesus in his. It must not serve to defend the status quo, neither in the social order nor in the church.

The proposal to pursue christology within the context of ethics does not require at the outset a formal system of ethics. It is enough to begin by defining ethics as that realm of life which has to do with matters of conscience. It therefore includes the social formation of conscience, its occasional transformation in the individual and society, and the problems inherent in acting conscientiously. The terms "ethical" and "ethics" in this book refer to one or more of these aspects of conscience.

I have said earlier that conscience is the distinguishing characteristic of human beings. Ethical religions such as Judaism and Christianity are devoted to that kind of worship of God which heightens the awareness of conscience and seeks the fulfillment of its demands for justice. A major difference between Judaism and Christianity has been their disparate understandings of the role played by Jesus in this process. Following Paul's argument in Romans, Christians have usually said that Christ brings freedom from "the law." If so, it is a strange freedom, for it neither puts an end to conscience nor removes the expectation that we shall all be judged. The whole of Christian theology and preaching about salvation by grace has not been able to supplant, if indeed it was supposed to, the vision of the Last Judgment depicted by Jesus in Matthew 25:31–46, wherein the sheep are divided from the goats according to their acts of love for poor people and prisoners. "By their fruits you shall know them" (Matt. 7:20). It is true that Jesus sat loose to many particular religious laws, but he added very demanding obligations having especially to do with concern for the destitute. He seems to have taught that one's conscience should be radicalized. In this may be found both the anarchistic impulse I noted some pages above and also a very sharp ethic of healing and liberation. According to Jesus, it is no purpose of God that people should suffer.

The suffering of Jesus on the cross, his resurrection after death, and the failure of the world of God to make its appearance led Christians gradually to regard the death of Jesus as some kind of divine transaction with evil that had mysteriously broken all evil power in the world. In other words, the burden of the radicalized conscience was transferred back to God. The result, as far as ethics is concerned, was twofold: (1) The ethical conscience of Christians became secondary to the salvific work of God in Christ; (2) Jesus as the Christ became the model of the good person, for he was now understood to have been "perfect." The stage was set for the interpretation of Christian ethics as *"imitatio Christi,"* which is with us today in popular form as the question, "What would Jesus do?"

While it is beyond my powers as a historian to document the point, I suspect it might be shown that the two ethical "results" of early christology I have mentioned were, in fact, the motivating source of the christology and not the other way around. I am thinking that my methodological proposal to locate christology within ethics and not prior to it is in fact what has always gone on in the history of theology. Our human situation, I suggest, is such that we cannot avoid adopting some ethical stance or another in the situations in which we find ourselves. This necessity, and the ideas we form of what actions are good, underlie and shape our teaching about Christ. The question, "Who is Jesus?" is a mirror question: Whatever we answer reveals the state of our conscience. In this sense, which is an exceedingly important one, Jesus is not the source of Christian conscience and not the form or content of it, but he instead reveals it for what it is. The attempt of Christians to hide their conscience behind Jesus, making him responsible for their decisions and looking to him to forgive moral failure, does not fool the world. Actions and failures to act which cannot be justified by conscience cannot be justified by Christ either. Nor by God. To put God above conscience amounts to putting God below it. Nothing can be better than what is good. If my conscience is dull, unenlightened, weak from too many rationalizations, it can be improved. But this is only to say that I come to have more conscience, not less. As Jesus seems to have understood when he summarized all the law and the prophets in the twin commandments to love God and love one's neighbor, love makes conscience more acute.

Since ethics is the beginning and the ending of christology, the christological task is to define the role of Christ in the fulfillment of individual and social conscience. The method suggested here is to view Christ as a *party* to ethical development, not as its norm or its completion. Far from being outside or above the ethical history of the world, Christ is radically within it. This means that Christ also has an ethical history and is not forever the same. We should be prepared to meet Christ in forms not predicted in the New Testament. The doctrine of the Incarnation, far from indicating that God has assumed forever the form of the Nazarene, should suggest that we may yet encounter God in ways that offend in order to make radical our present-future conscience.

Second, christological formulation requires freedom from the past in order to generate a freedom in the present for the sake of the future. Whatever the role of tradition may be in Christian life, it should not be that of setting definite limits to what can or should be said in the present regarding Christ and the future. I am far from wishing or advocating any "escape from history," but I do want Christianity to free itself from regarding its tradition as sacred. In the way that the Bible and the creedal and sacramental traditions are treated in church and seminary, I detect a frequent idolatry of the "given" past. This often works, ironically, to decrease one's knowledge of what has in fact been said and done in Christian history. How many defenders of "the tradition of priestly celibacy," for example, are aware that celibacy did not become the general practice of the priesthood until it was forced upon the secular clergy by a newly monasticized papacy in the eleventh and twelfth centuries? (Barstow 1979).

Christology is especially subject to the tyranny of tradition, because the church fears to tamper with doctrines concerning its "Lord." It is more nearly acceptable to proclaim a Christian atheism than to cast doubt upon the eternal validity of Jesus, as the Death of God theology a decade ago demonstrated. The method I propose holds that what has traditionally been taught about Christ does not govern what should be taught now. Furthermore, the method would eliminate all formulae and phrasings that bind the church to its own past in the name of Jesus. For example, we should not speak of the atoning work of Christ as having been performed "once, for all," or to say, as does the Book of Common Prayer, that Jesus "made there a once, perfect . . . sacrifice for the sins of the whole world." If a work of salvation has been perfected in the past, it is either irrelevant to our present-future ethical action or else is determinative of what we should think and do. Similar objection has to be made to christological concepts like "final revelation," "center of history," and so on. Precisely because Jesus was a person of history, our teaching about Christ should avoid concepts that elevate one particular time of history to permanence. Intellectual honesty in the twentieth century requires a thoroughgoing historical relativism, to which no christology of which I am aware has well addressed itself. The method here proposed requires an attempt to do so.

Third, christological formulation requires understanding existence as relationship. Nothing exists, not even God, except in relation to something else: Nothing has its existence alone. Martin Buber's "In the beginning is the relation," provides a basis for christological reflection. The relation Buber had in mind was between a human being and God, which he saw adumbrated in I-Thou encounters among human persons, but Buber's point is as philosophical as it is religious. He proposes that reality does not begin with any individual entity but with a relationship. From this point of view, strange as it seems to our usual logic, to ask what an entity is "prior" to its being-in-relation is as absurd as Augustine said it was to inquire what God did "before" he created time (*Confessions,* Book XI). We are taught to think that counting begins with the number *one,* to which other numbers are added, but the case is that the number *one* has no meaning except in relation to all other numbers. The beginning of *one* is the relation of *many.* Such a thought was, in fact, basic to Christian trinitarian thinking in early times, but its special implications for christology seem not to have been carried through. Perhaps the task has been left to us who are born into the age of Einsteinian relativity. What this means, in brief, is that christology will have to avoid terms that insist upon the singularity of Christ, replacing them with terms conveying mutuality of relation. Terms such as "the only begotten Son," "King," "High Priest," "Bridegroom," "Savior," and (perhaps) "Messiah" connote "the one and only." They all imply that Christ is himself alone and is unique. They obscure the vital point that the reality of Christ is a relation of mutual dependence, an I-Thou relation. While the titles of Christ I have mentioned do suggest certain relationships, these relations are not mutual. The titles depict the dependence of an inferior upon a superior, which is the result of their having been chosen to help maintain civil and religious order. It is true that to call Christ the Lord in the time of the Roman Empire meant that Caesar was *not* Lord, which Rome regarded as seditious. By the same token, however, it meant that the Christian should obey Christ, which soon meant to obey the elders of the Church, so that the Church acquired a tribal character. I am not so simplistic as to think there was nothing good or necessary in this. I do not expect perfection in my ancestors, and this frees me to respect their achievements. I am suggesting, however, that obedience, whether to church authorities, to secular powers, or to Christ, is not a sufficient virtue to inform a christology for our time. Even if it could be shown that what Jesus wanted was obedience, which hardly seems a good interpretation of discipleship, it would not necessarily follow that obedience is what we owe him today (cf. Sölle 1970).

Since the concept of reality as mutual relation is so important in the method proposed, I shall look for terms to describe Jesus which connote it. Scripture and tradition are by no means devoid of these. Among them are "friend," "teacher" (rabbi), "servant" (helper), and "brother." Each of these suggests and invites some form of mutual solidarity between Jesus and those who belong to him. It is possible that "Messiah" is another such term, but that depends on how the word is taken. However, we are not limited to the received tradition nor to scripture in our search for authentic christological names. Our process is the same as that which went on in the writing of the New Testament and has continued ever since in Christian literature, preaching, and teaching: to find the names that convey the effect Jesus has upon us and the relation created between us and him.

To find the right word for the actual experience is, at heart, an artistic achievement. It is often fulfilled by ordinary people who are not ashamed to express the plain truth of what has happened to them. Great honesty is required, for it is all too easy to slip into the cliches of an expected piety. When these are jumped over by a leap of imaginative faith, the result can be shocking. Such seems to have been the case when Peter replied to Jesus' question, "Who do you say that I am?" with the words, "You are the Christ, the Son of the living God" (Matt. 16:16). Jesus flinched at this. He accused Peter of being a tempter and told him to tell no one what he had said. I draw attention not so much to the words of Peter's formula as to the tremulously creative leap he took in their utterance.

It is possible that to call Jesus the Christ, the Son of the living God, has again become a satanic temptation. And perhaps this is also true of any other names we might apply. Easy Jesus-talk is next door to devil-talk and may raise up spirits of evil, especially if the very name of Jesus is understood to have divine power. To guard against this, we have to keep ever in mind that all language about Jesus, including the pages of the New Testament, refers to an actual person who is only partly comprehended in whatever is said of him. This testifies not to his divinity but to his human activity. What we seek, then, is language adequate to convey some crucial aspects of his relation to his contemporaries and to us. Scripturalists maintain that this has been definitively achieved in the language of the New Testament, which cannot and must not be superseded. Even the scripturalists themselves, however, do not follow this rule, for they are driven by the necessity of preaching to invent new phrasings in testimony to the Jesus they proclaim. This inevitable procedure is taken, in the method I propose, as having important christological meaning. What people say about Jesus has a definite bearing on who Jesus was and is. Who he "really" was cannot be a matter of dogmatic finality because Jesus' reality lies in transactions *between* him and whoever speaks of him, including the historian. Albert Schweitzer showed this clearly in his great book on *The Quest of the Historical Jesus* (1906). Those who demand certainty and fixed conclusions of history, who include some scholarly historians as well as all believers in the inerrancy of scripture, were disheartened by the historical scepticism of Schweitzer's book. What it positively showed, however, is that a relational bond exists between Jesus and his interpreters. It is not as if the latter simply projected their own interests onto a neutral, wholly passive, surface called "Jesus." It is rather that Jesus *responds* to our interests within certain limits, and with certain characteristics our projections do not anticipate. The give-and-take between interest and response forms the story of Jesus and the reality that bears his name.

To refuse to regard Christ as a being unique in all time and space does not mean reduction of Christ to the human average. To say that something is not unique does not mean that it has no special character or importance. It only means that the importance, the function, and the quality are realized in a relation of mutual affect. Hence, it would become as true to say that humanity is the savior of Christ as to say the opposite. Indeed, this idea raises some of the most crucial questions the church can ask today: Is Christ worth saving? If so, why? What follows for our behavior and our future life? How, by what strategies, can Christian people save Christ from the oblivion into which so many of religion's gods and heroes have fallen? Should we try?

Fourth, the church's teaching about Christ today must include a reevaluation of both the "scriptural Jesus" and the "historical Jesus."

Among those who take seriously the historical research of the New Testament, there is a widespread assumption that the norm of our christological assertions should be the "historical Jesus," whom they think should take precedence over the rather confusing figure so variously depicted in the books of the New Testament (Küng 1976; Sobrino 1976; and others). I regard any such assumption as naïve historicism and oppose it as a method. It is as faulty in its own way as is naive scripturalism in another. Common to both are two errors: (1) the idea that in scripture or in historical reconstruction we encounter something for which we ourselves are not responsible, but which is nevertheless "true" and therefore normative; (2) the supposition that a christological norm is to be found in some record of the past.

The early Christians chose to regard the history and scriptures of Israel as prologue to the "main event" in Jesus, whereas the Jews who did not convert regarded their history and scriptures as prologue to an event which had not yet occurred and for which they would continue to wait in messianic expectation. The issue for christology today is whether the "main event" is to be regarded as having already occurred in the first century or is to be seen as taking place in our own present-future.

The method I propose subordinates the events and literature surrounding Jesus' life in Palestine in the first century to the actions of God in our own present-future. Discernment of present-future actions of God is here held to be normative for faith and christology. Hence, no historical documents are normative, and neither is the fruit of any research concerning them. Scriptural documents and the scientific investigation of them remain very important, because they provide ever new information about the memoried context in which we live and act. Faith, however, is not properly lodged in memory, nor in historical fact, nor in any kind of legacy. A faith that is liberating and life-giving finds itself devoted to a subject having power in the present-future. As the followers of Jesus discovered, the continuity of the subject (Jesus or God) with its past, or they with theirs, is a secondary matter. A sense of historical continuity helps keep one sane, but it is not a matter of faith, which has always to do with a radical experience of the present coupled with radical expectations for the future. For this phenomenon of faith we use such terms as "renewal," "conversion," and "being born again." The genuine subject of these experiences, I propose, is God. The subject (some would say object) of Christian faith is not Jesus of Nazareth but God. I am driving at two points:

a. Christology has most to do with what we affirm about God, to which all affirmation about Christ should be secondary.

b. Christology is ever in danger of valuing the past more highly than the present-future. Of this danger my method aims to steer as clear as possible. The way to do it, I think, is to regard the past, including the life, death, and resurrection of Jesus, as "prologue to the present act."

Fifth, as the "scriptural Jesus" and the "historical Jesus" should both be re-valued in christology, so should the formulae in christological tradition. The authority of these does not come from the fact that the church has previously affirmed them. Such authority as they should have comes from the light they shed upon actions of God discerned in our present-future. They are to be used as aids in that discernment and not to define the limits of what we may teach about Christ.

Finally, as we have the obligation to discern the actions of God in our present-future, we must also discern what the resurrected Christ is doing today. However tenuous and controversial this may be, christology may not avoid it. On our left are those who think that Christ is dead and buried, having nothing to do with life today except as superstition and false ideology. On our right are persons and groups who claim everything for Jesus, invoking the name to bless every piece of luck to come their way. And behind us are the many conventional Christians who vaguely suppose that Christ is still doing whatever it is "he" has always done. The church, insofar as it is honest, should find a more genuine assessment of the present activity of Christ. It must ask what our situation would be if Christ were not active in it. To do this is very difficult. It is even more difficult, as I have already suggested, than to ask where we would be without God. The latter question was asked by Dietrich Bonhoeffer in his *Letters and Papers From Prison* (1967), and many other Christians have asked it since. But the "death of God" people have not, to my knowledge, asked where we would be without Jesus. They seem to take it for granted that "he" is with us. Perhaps, but we must ask if this is so. What is the evidence? Where the present-future activity of Christ is experientially absent, no amount of recitation of the creeds convinces listeners that the Christ referred to is living. Jesus himself said, "By their fruits you shall know them" (Matt. 7:20). This is the rule by which all religious beliefs can be best evaluated, and it applies to Christ today. We are not to seek the living Christ among the dead.

My intention in this book, however, is not to provide here and now a clear image of the living Christ. A reader who would turn the following pages in search of a fully developed picture of Christ will not find it. There are two reasons for not giving it.

In the first place, I wish to honor by the example of my own reticence a similar hesitation which will be felt in the presence of this challenge by every sensitive Christian. We pause, wondering by what authority the fantasies of our own imagination are to be taken seriously in the body of Christ. The knowledge that every generation and every cultural group of Christians have envisioned a somewhat different Christ induces in us ambivalence. Perhaps the task should be left to mystics, artists, inspired preachers, and other visionaries.

In the second place, as my final chapter will indicate, I believe that the proper place for the envisionment of Christ today is within the worshipping community, and more by oral than by written expression. The authority to re-envision Christ does not belong to any individual alone, even though the testimony of individuals is necessary. A communitarian ethic and christology such as that proposed here requires that the Christ of the church shall be a composite of the experiences and expectations of all who gather in Christ's name, not only of those who are priests, preachers, theologians, and others gifted with office and fine words. A major purpose of this book and its method is to empower those expectant ones in the churches who are most dispossessed. I know, however, that I do not write in their language. I therefore direct my attention to the clearing away of certain old assumptions and familiar teachings that inhibit all of us from seeking Christ in our knowledge of the present and our expectation of the future. In the last three chapters I shall go beyond critique to the beginnings of a new envisionment, but my proposals there will be suggestive rather than definitive. In the end, for better or worse, the appeal is to the ethical expectations of the gathered community insofar as it is open to the power of God.

·3·

Critique of Christ as Center, Model, and Norm

As most people have come to know it, Christianity means putting Christ at the center of life. This is a thought to be found not only in simple piety but also in scholarly christologies. In Jesus, it is often said, a Christian is to see the perfect exemplar of humanity, and therefore the normative model of ethical Christian life. By implication, this norm extends to all life, and the church has long taught that Christ Jesus is the true center of the temporal world. It is my task now to critique this honored idea, since it no longer corresponds to the lives Christians do or should lead.

Biblical scholarship has drawn attention to the fact that the New Testament is mostly a collection of messianic writings. Messiahs, self-proclaimed or designated such by their disciples, appeared with great frequency in Palestine in those days. As far as we can tell, Jesus shared with many of his compatriots a messianic expectation. It is not clear that he thought of himself as Messiah, but others certainly regarded him that way. His disciples, the early church, St. Paul, and most other New Testament writers interpreted Jesus' ministry, death, and resurrection to mean that the kingdom of God would arrive within their lifetime. Those who believed in him thought he would promptly return from heaven to establish the reign of God on earth which he had foretold. Given such a belief, all "things of this world" — that is, things as they are — became of minor significance. Their day was nearly over.

Twenty centuries later, we find it hard to imagine how such thoughts went through the early Christians' heads. To grasp it, we have to think of "cargo cults" on South Pacific islands and in parts of Africa, where self-appointed leaders spring up promising health and wealth to everyone because the secrets of how to get "cargo" are about to be revealed to them (Harris 1974; cf. Kee 1977).

Hearing such fanciful messages, we must remember that we are listening to the near-desperate hopes of oppressed people. Battered down, exploited for their labor, taxed out of most of their earnings, brutalized in ways both subtle and violent, oppressed people often lay claim to their protesting hope by believing in promises of divine deliverance, sudden and soon. In Jesus' day, Palestine was a breeding ground of such expectations. The kingdom of God was not a remote thought. It was as urgent as the survival of one's own child, and this for very clear historical reasons.

The homeland of Jesus was a colony of the Roman Empire. The Herodian kings were puppet rulers propped up by their Roman overlords. Most of the population were extremely poor, living by subsistence farming, a few crafts, and day labor. Their lot became worse each year, since the policy of Rome and the Herods was to bleed them with taxes. As we are informed in the Gospel of Luke (2:1–2), the whole country was "required to be enrolled." Lest we suppose that compliance with this tax registration was merely a matter of good civic duty, we must know that the people were up in arms about it. During the years between 4 B.C.E. and 70 C.E., when the Romans finally quelled a major revolt, Judaea was the scene of constant guerilla warfare. To maintain its control, the mighty Roman Empire had to bring in battalions of its best troops, commanded by the foremost generals in the empire. It sent Pontius Pilate to be the colonial governor because of his reputation for ruthless efficiency. In the end, Rome put the rebellion down by destroying the whole nation. The temple at Jerusalem was put to the fire (70 C.E.); most of the entire population were driven into exile. These severe measures, as well as the seventy-five years it took Rome to pacify the country, speak clearly of the degree of resistance the people of Judaea offered to their oppressors.

The people who first heard and responded to Jesus were, like him, poor people oppressed on their own land, desperate for deliverance. To call Jesus "Messiah" in such a time was to see him as their liberator, one who could, in the name of God, release them from political and economic captivity. They did not look for a merely "religious" liberation, nor simply for forgiveness of sin, release from the burdens of ritual laws, or an eased conscience before God. Although such matters were surely involved, they took their importance from the political context, the daily hope of rescue from tyranny.

That the New Testament was written from an eschatalogical point of view was rediscovered for modern readers by Albert Schweitzer in *The Quest of the Historical Jesus* (1906). The book demonstrated that the gospels cannot be the basis for any history of Jesus' life because their information does not lie in a biographical direction. Instead, the earliest gospels proclaim the end of an age (its last days, its *eschaton*) and the coming of a new one by the intervention of God. The synoptic Evangelists drew a picture of Jesus only to communicate his miracles, his message, and his messianic status. The same eschatological preoccupation belonged to Jesus as well, Schweitzer concluded. The eschatalogical orientation of Jesus and the Evangelists is so different from that of our culture that we cannot reconstruct from the documents a Jesus whose character and deeds we might understand as both credible and realistic—that is, a "historical" Jesus.

Since Schweitzer, there have been renewed attempts to research the "historical Jesus." A "new quest" was undertaken some years ago, but has not proved successful (J. M. Robinson 1959). We should remind ourselves that the Christian religion has never depended on knowing Jesus "as he actually was." Ever since St. Paul successfully claimed to have known Jesus in a manner just as authentic as those who had walked with him in Galilee and Judaea, the "truly historical" Jesus, whatever he was like, has given way to a Jesus of confessional testimony. The church is not founded upon the particulars of a historical person about whose acts and words we might fruitfully debate, but upon what has come to be called "the Christ of faith." Since "Christ" means messiah or deliverer, and since faith (as the Epistle to the Hebrews says) means the basis of what is hoped for (Hebrews 11:1), we may understand that the early

Christian community was formed around its belief that Jesus would, with God, bring deliverance from all forms of subjugation.

During most of its subsequent life, the church has assumed that the mystery surrounding the figure of Jesus in the New Testament is due to his "divine nature." A being who is "Very God of Very God" can be expected to be inscrutable. Assuming the divinity of Jesus, the church had no reason to spend time and energy investigating historically his human nature. In fact, the church resisted such investigation when scholars began to pursue it in the eighteenth century, for the church accurately saw that to study Jesus historically required one to set methodically to the side all regard of Jesus as divine, semidivine, or supernatural.

The contribution of Schweitzer was to show that even if one does set aside the divinity of Jesus, even if one works from strictly human historical assumptions, the mystery remains. With his eschatological vision of the kingdom of God intact, Jesus becomes a historical curiosity about whom little can be known except what the gospels, with all their contradictions, already say. Without his eschatological vision, Jesus vanishes into the thin air of speculation.

This, in brief sketch, is the situation in which we find ourselves, and the theological problem is to decide where to locate the increasingly opaque figure of Jesus with respect to our understanding of God and human history. I shall bluntly say that I do not think we may longer pretend that Jesus is our starting point. When I say this, I am remembering Karl Barth's insistence that all theological knowledge is based upon the revelation of God in Christ, so that theology must necessarily take a christological point of departure (Barth 1936–1969, Vol. I, Part I, pp. 124–135). I am thinking, too, of popular Christian piety expressed in hymns like the famous one by Charles Wesley: "The Church's One Foundation Is Jesus Christ Her Lord." I am thinking of sacramental Christianity, conspicuously in Roman Catholicism, eastern Orthodoxy, and high-church Anglicanism, in which the sacrament of the body and blood of Christ is fundamental. I am thinking of a kind of evangelicalism that often begins and ends its mission by calling upon sinners to "come to Jesus." I am thinking of the theology of Paul Tillich, which, for all its dialectical subtlety, is based squarely upon the paradox of the unity of "God-manhood" in Jesus as the Christ. And I am thinking, more sympathetically, of the warning years ago from H. Richard Niebuhr that the Christian religion is in danger of turning Jesus into an idol, worshipping him as one ought to worship God (H. R. Niebuhr 1943).

Standing athwart most of the theological, sacramental, and evangelical traditions of the church, I must be careful not to say that all of it has been wrong from the start. The christological error I am about to describe may not always have been as serious as it is today. Perhaps it was never totally erroneous: Few things are. We deal always with mixtures of truth and error. As time and circumstance change, flaws and potential flaws in our thinking can become more serious than they once were. In the sciences this leads now and again to what Thomas Kuhn has called "paradigm-shifts," radically new ways of envisioning the data we are trying to comprehend (Kuhn 1962). I believe the church needs today a paradigm-shift in its christology. The need for it has been growing since the age of Enlightenment. The presence of liberalism and modernism in the church has made the need acute. One may see this dramatically in the tensions within Roman Catholicism since Vatican II. Today, theologies of hope, of liberation, and of women's religious experiences are putting the received christology of the tradition into crisis. I believe that unless we can break out of our old paradigm, the church will founder. God may require a new instrument.

When Jesus the Messiah did not return in the first century C.E. to end the old epoch and institute the new, the church that had expected him to do so made a paradigm-shift. This story is familiar to students of that period, but it has not yet been heard by the inner ear of the church. Until it is, we shall remain stuck, for we shall continue to imagine that the way we think of Jesus as the Christ is the way he has always been seen. Not realizing that the paradigm-shift in the early church was even greater than the changes effected, say, by Thomas Aquinas in the thirteenth century and Martin Luther in the sixteenth, we attribute more consistency to belief about Jesus than in fact there has been.

The story of the early paradigm-shift has recently been told by Rosemary Ruether in her book about Christian anti-Semitism, *Faith and Fratricide* (1974). Her depiction of the shift is especially valuable because she has shown its disastrous ethical consequences for the attitude of Christians to Jews ever since. I am in full agreement with Ruether that any doctrine which reduces one's ethical sensibility must have within it something quite wrong, and this has surely been the case in the impact of christology upon the ethics of Christianity toward Jews and Judaism. Ruether's book is quite persuasive on the point that Christianity's attitude toward Jews has spilled over into racism and sexism.

The early church, about one generation after the departure of Jesus, had to face a serious question: "If Jesus was, as we believe, the Messiah of God, and if he has not, as we expected, brought the kingdom of God to pass, in what sense was he and is he the Messiah?" Tension between what was expected of a Messiah and what had in fact happened (or not happened) was so great that something had to yield. Christians could either give up believing in Jesus as Messiah or they could change their messianic concept. They did the latter.

To account for this change, I think we have to consider three factors. First, surely, is the hold of Jesus on the imagination of the Christian communities. They were meeting, some of them daily, in fellowship devoted to his name. They ate in company with him as unseen guest. Many had pooled their property, placing their whole identity in the community devoted to Jesus' return. They sang new hymns and recited stories of his miraculous words and deeds. In short, they were Jesus people who had found a focus for their hope, a hope they had ceased to entrust to the workings of society or to religion as they had formerly known it.

Second, the Christian communities had formed and maintained their identity in deep controversy with their own kinspeople. Flying in the face of common sense, upsetting Jewish tradition concerning the Messiah, and opposing the living authorities within Judaism, the Jewish Christians had sown dissension within their native household of faith. We can imagine how great was the psychological and moral investment necessary to do this. Clear indications of it are to be found in the Fourth Gospel's frequent references to "the Jews," which means, of course, "those *other* Jews, the ones who have not, like us, believed that Jesus is the Messiah." It would be a humiliating thing to acknowledge, after much bitter controversy, that the messianic hopes fastened upon Jesus had been wrong.

I mention this second factor not only because it is so plausible historically but also because it remains with us to this day. One strong reason a christological paradigm-shift is so difficult now is that it cannot be entertained without humiliation. Can our belief in the Christ of faith have been wrong? If so, what becomes of our Christian identity and our continuity with "the faith of our fathers"? Behind such questions lurks what I may call the "specter" of the Jews, who all these centuries have existed as the sorest reminder to Christians that their christological affirmations are in some quarters anathema. The church is disturbed in its soul to think that in some way the Jews may have been right after all. To protect ourselves from this thought, we usually adhere all the more firmly to our familiar christological paradigm, believing that its "revealed" truth somehow justifies the price we have to pay, and the Jews have to pay, for our mutual alienation. In good times, we cooperate with Jews as best we can. In bad times, hostility breaks out with catastrophic ferocity, clear indication of the wound in our relationship that has festered from the church's inception. I am saying that christology has been (and still is) in significant part a defense of Christianity against Judaism. I am not saying we should therefore do away with it, which would be an absurd position. I am saying we should look again at the form and content of our christology, to see if there is a way we could responsibly change it, let it be refashioned by the grace of God, so as to bring us closer than we have dreamed toward fellowship with the "people of God" whom, from their point of view, we so long ago betrayed and have, from anyone's point of view, so often put to the fire. I have it in my mind—let this be judged as it will—that if the church were to rectify its relation to Judaism, it could compellingly renew the hope it may offer to all who suffer in the world. That is to say, the church might become more useful to God.

The third factor involved in the early church's paradigm-shift concerning the Christ lay in relation to the non-Jewish world. Christian messianism, by the latter part of the first century, was gaining acceptance in small groups all around the Mediterranean. The New Testament epistles were written to some of these groups. It seems clear that Jewish and Gentile elements were mixed in many of these congregations. What was becoming evident was that Christianity had a future within Hellenistic culture throughout the wide-flung Roman Empire—and even beyond, if we credit the legends of missionary travel to southern Asia. In this situation, Christians had every reason to interpret their *Christos* in ways that would appeal to persons who had never had a messianic tradition.

To reach such ears, it was necessary to mute the theme of messianic hope. It was more pertinent to play up another theme, that of a God-man who stood at the center of things. The culture in those days, which we call Hellenistic, was as pluralistic, as much of a jumble of this, that, and the other, as is world culture today. Rome ruled over peoples as different as ever the British Empire did, as varied as those around the world today who do business with Citibank, use VW cars, or listen to SONY radios. In other words, a canopy of trade and empire had been thrown over the most disparate languages, cultures, histories, and practices. Everyone knew that the canopy of empire, like the canopy of business and technology today, served merely to mask an underlying confusion. The real question was: What's it all about? Where is the center of value? Christianity rushed to answer this question, and just at the time when the Roman answer—worship of the Emperor—was proving itself so shallow. Christians began to say that the center of *everything*—culture, power, history, value, truth, and human kinship— was the God-man Jesus.

As it turned out, most of the known world was just about ready for such a message, which took hold in widely separated places. It spread underground like vines in a garden, outcropping where it could. When the emperor Constantine was converted in the early fourth century and adopted the cross of Christ as his sign of victory, the weeds became the flowers. The stone the builders had rejected became indeed the cornerstone. This has lasted, in Europe and the Americas it colonized, until a few years ago; but the Christian cornerstone of Western culture is now dislodged. The cultural edifice built upon it will not last much longer.

We who have grown up in Christendom find it difficult to know what to make of Jesus if he is not the center. We are taught to put him at the center of our lives. We are taught to regard him as the center of the church and the center of culture, publicly acknowledged or not. We are told by theologians that he is the center of history. Insofar as we are Christians, our thought is supposed to be *centered on* Jesus. This is the legacy we have inherited in the church from a paradigm-shift in thinking about Jesus that took place toward the end of the first century. The shift was to move the Messiah from the *lead edge* of history to its *center*. At the lead edge, he was a herald of the future. At the center he became the embodiment of a humanity already made perfect in God. As Rosemary Ruether has cogently put it, eschatological hopes were read back into the Jesus who had already come, so that instead of being the one who led into the *eschaton* Jesus became the one who had already fulfilled it in his own person (Ruether 1974, pp. 246ff.).

Asking themselves how Jesus could be the Messiah without having ushered in the kingdom of God, Christians near the end of the first century began to reply that Jesus was *in himself* the kingdom. If you put *him* at the center, you had already arrived. There was, to be sure, the promise of his second coming and his eventual rule of the entire world. That promise would still be fulfilled, but not soon. It would come long hence, at "the end of time." Meanwhile, everything that it represents is *already* known and imparted to the faithful by that Jesus who was and ever shall be the very incarnation of God.

The church moved then toward what Ruether calls "an illegitimate historicizing of the eschatalogical" (p. 248). Jesus came to be thought of as having fulfilled the promises of God in his own person. As the center of history, he stood also for its beginning and end. The kingdom of Heaven became a fellowship or communion with Jesus, who now became equally present in and equally distant from all times and places. The community of his fellowship, the church, came to be spoken of as his body. Little by little, the church came to regard itself as the kingdom of God on earth, flawed in fact but perfect in principle. Latent here was the thought that the church, being the universal body of Christ the center, could do no wrong. This thought gradually shaped policy and led to ideas supporting the inherent (eventually "infallible") authority of the Vicar of Christ.

When Protestantism broke away from the authoritative claims of

Rome in the sixteenth century, it did not change the paradigm of Christ the center. It simply moved the place where the center was supposed to be identified: from the sacramental priesthood and the teaching office of the church at Rome to the pages of Holy Scripture. As a Protestant, I think this was healthy at the start, for it broke the monopoly on Christian authority held in Europe by the Roman church. To hold the supremacy of "God's Written Word" over the head of the Pope, as Luther did, was to create a new dynamism in the church, to open it to historical change as it had not been open for centuries. Alas, this move ceased rather soon to be radical, and especially not in christology. In our own century, Paul Tillich could rightly speak of the continued dependence of "the Protestant principle" upon a "religious substance" that is more clearly evident in the Catholic church than in Protestantism (Tillich 1948, pp. 192-205 and 222-233). That substance is the affirmation of Christ as the center of all things, and the sacramental theology that comes from it.

Martin Luther, building upon an Augustinian heritage, interpreted Christ as the center and substance of the Bible. All scripture was understood to speak of Christ, in whom the prophecies and promises of the Old Testament were fulfilled. This kind of scriptural interpretation was, of course, ancient. It can be discerned in the use some New Testament writers make of the Old. What was new was Luther's placing of the Bible, with Christ as *its* center, at the center of the church and the Christian life. This meant that the Bible would itself soon acquire the attribute of perfection that had previously been claimed by the teaching office of the Roman Catholic church. Luther did not intend this. His interpretive principle of a Christ-centered scripture, further refined by his insistence that the message of Christ is "justification by faith," allowed him a scale of value by which to judge in scripture those parts which lay closer to the center, those further away, and some so remote that Luther said they were not binding upon Christians.

Nevertheless, by Luther's teaching, the Bible moved into the center of the church, bearing as its own center the perfect Christ. Before the sixteenth century was out, Protestant orthodoxy came in with its credo that the Bible is in all parts authoritative. The motive was a desire for doctrinal certainty, combined with the assumption that there has to be somewhere a center of perfection. If the teaching of Rome was no longer the center and no longer certain, where was the certain center to be found? Answer: in Christ. Where was *he* to be found? Answer: in the Bible, of which he is heart, soul, and most visible subject. Therefore, the Bible could do no wrong.

I am presenting what I take to have been the logic of the development. In fact, the argument was usually stated from the premise that *God* can do no wrong. The scriptures were said to have been verbally inspired by God. However, the hermeneutic employed by Protestant orthodoxy was and is christocentric, and this seems to me to display the underlying logic at work.

Some of my readers inherit or are caught up in a Protestant tradition that has led, today as yesterday, to insistence upon the inerrancy of scripture (cf. Lindsell 1976). Others, identifying with liberal thought, will imagine themselves to be free of this albatross. My own heritage in these matters is mostly (not entirely) liberal, and I teach in a seminary that acquired its modern posture and reputation in a famous case that had to do with questions of biblical truth. That was the heresey trial in 1892 of Professor Charles A. Briggs in the Presbyterian Church, U.S.A. He was a "modernist" scholar, and Union Theological Seminary sided with him against its own Presbyterian connections, becoming independent of church control, committed to a liberal interpretation of scripture, essentially ridding itself of the question of biblical inerrancy. Or so it hoped. The question refuses to die.

I speak now to those who do not like to take seriously the question of scriptural inerrancy. The reason it continues to haunt even liberal theology is to be found in the christological paradigm, the underlying matter which gives rise to the presenting question of the inerrancy of scripture. There are many ways to approach the subject. I choose the one that has to do with history and historical methods of scholarship (on which I touch again in Chapter 5).

Liberal Christianity in the nineteenth and twentieth centuries (to go no further back) does not seem to have addressed itself to a basic question which may be phrased like this: Can the idea of an enduring *center* of all things, including history, be compatible with the sense of "history" that is presupposed in modern historical scholarship? I think the answer to this question must be negative, but I do not hear this plainly from biblical, ecclesiastical, or theological historians. Specifically, I do not hear them to say that since Christ is a historical concept referring to a historical person, then Christ must be a *movable* and *relative* figure, like all other historical phenomena. (For a good exposition of the principle of relativity in modern thinking, see Harvey 1966.) Instead of this, I hear that "Jesus of Nazareth" is a historical figure, known only in the relativistic way that all history is known, but that "Christ" is somehow above history—transcendent in such a way as to be not truly a subject of historical inquiry or judgment. This, I have long thought, is to have it both ways. It is no wonder that more conservative Christians have thought we liberals exhibit bad faith.

We have indeed been in a posture of bad faith, I am coming to think, because we have not understood (or been willing to risk saying) that christologies putting Christ at the *center* of things are mistaken. So powerful is the symbolism of "centers," and so ancient is this symbolism in the church, that our imaginations have failed us when we have come near the thought that God might have no investment in any kind of enduring center. Protestantism has long taught that God has no need of a geographical center, such as a temple or a holy city at Rome, Jerusalem, or Mecca. Yet we have not been taught that God has also no need of a temporal or historical center. On the contrary, my generation learned that to think of Christ as the center of history (not space, mind you, but history) was essential. We learned this from Karl Barth, Oscar Cullmann, Reinhold Niebuhr, T. S. Eliot, W. H. Auden, C. S. Lewis, and even process theologians like D. D. Williams and Norman Pittenger. Perhaps we are supposed to have learned better by now, yet I find the idea of a christic center of history and experience present equally in theologians of my own generation—in Van Harvey (1966), Langdon Gilkey (1976), Richard R. Niebuhr (1972), John Cobb (1975), David Tracy (1975), and so on. The same is true in Jürgen Moltmann's *Theology of Hope* (1967) for all its concern with the future, and is, if anything, even more true of his *The Crucified God* (1974). As for the theologies of liberation and also the black theologies, none of them has yet, to my knowledge, conceived of a Christ who is not the center, model, or norm of humanity. Even Jon Sobrino's very provocative *Christology at the Crossroads* (1976) regards the example of Jesus as normative for Christian discipleship.

If liberal Christian theology were to set out, as I am doing, to displace Christ from the center of things, it would surely know the same two fears that pursue me: (1) Will I not come out in no place at all, lost in a wilderness of historical relativity? (2) Will not the churches either ignore me or tear me to pieces, both the liberal ones I have accused of bad faith and the conservative ones only too delighted to find what apostasy we liberals have had in the back of our minds all along?

With such fears, one doesn't need enemies. One needs a kind of courage to be guided by the lure of things not often spoken, the silent promise of things to come.

Tremulous at this juncture, I am sure I would not dare say a word if I did not have as a burden on my mind some people in this world who do not have, and have never had as long as we can remember, any recognized authority to speak of Christ for themselves. I wish to remind my readers of persons and beings who have been rendered weak, invisible, or ashamed by the church's affirmation of Jesus Christ as center of all things:

1. Those who are not male, as is Christ, the center of all things.

2. Those who are neither white nor Semitic, as is Christ, the center of all things.

3. Those who are born without inheritance, unlike Christ, the center of all things.

4. Those who feel strongly their sexuality, unlike Christ, the center of all things.

5. Those who have never known, and do not wish to know, Abraham as their father, who have other fathers and mothers to honor, unlike Christ, the center of all things.

6. Those who have no community to surround them, unlike Christ, the center of all things.

7. Those who have never learned language, whose hopes are as mute as buds on a tree, unlike Christ the Word, the center of all things.

8. Those who are Jews and have never consented to believe that Jesus is the Christ, the center of all things, and have incurred the hatred of many who worshipped the center.

I speak simply. The Christ who has *already* come provides little hope for "outsiders." I maintain that what does not liberate them for the world of God does not liberate anyone of conscience. We look for another.

"Are you he that should come, or shall we look for another?" (Luke 7:19-20).

Let the answer given in those days be sufficient to those days. The faithful in that time responded in their expectation, and that was good for them. Yet Jesus himself once advised, "Let the dead bury their dead" (Matt. 8:22; Luke 9:60).

We face our own necessities. We know better than our ancestors the moral imperatives that press upon *us,* not *them.* If we solve our own problems by the rules our ancestors used to solve theirs, it is clear that we worship our ancestors, not a God who is able to change the very environment in which we live.

Where there is a fixed center of history, there is a known beginning and end. As it believes in a permanent center, a center in Christ already made known long ago, the church addicts itself to the habit of yesterday. Against this, the messianism of Judaea will ever and rightly oppose itself. It will keep the ancient law as witness to that future day when the last and true Messiah shall bring the shalom of God. The one they expect, the one Christians should expect, is not Jesus of Nazareth, not Christ past but Christ future.

It will seem, perhaps, that my intention is to repudiate Jesus Christ. This is not so, but I do think some kind of repudiation is necessary in order to break the power not of Christ but of the christocentric paradigm we have inherited. Struggle and repudiation of the sort I have in mind is not unknown to Christians of strong ethical conscience, who often experience the Christ they already know as a burden to be somehow cast off before they can encounter a new Christ in a more faithful, responsible life. A person who has never felt such tension has not, I think, taken Christian discipleship very seriously.

Struggle between Christ and conscience appears in the New Testament itself. It began in conflict between those who saw Jesus as the Messiah and those who did not, their reading of Torah having led them to expect a far different deliverer. These latter were not "blind" or "stubborn," as Christian polemic made them out to be; they were simply pursuing a different, and indeed a noble, ethic. The struggle was continued in debates within the young churches as to whether allegiance to Christ Jesus, who was himself circumcised, required the same of his followers. When Paul set aside the necessity of circumcision and Peter broke with Judaic dietary rules, they were repudiating known aspects of Jesus in order to envision something new in the risen Christ. Throughout the Christian era, similar controversy has arisen concerning slavery, marriage, priesthood, the establishment of Christianity as a state religion, the relation of the Holy Spirit to Christ (the *Filioque* argument that divided East from West), the idea of Christian capitalism (in the sixteenth century), Christian socialism (in the nineteenth and twentieth), and many other issues that have emerged in times of marked social change. In all of these one may discern a struggle between a Christ who is already known in scriptural tradition and a risen Christ, whose form is not yet visible and is therefore open to the judgment of conscience and ethical expectation.

Even so, theologians seldom question the premise that Christ is the norm and center of a Christian conscience. Holding fast to this, theology explains struggles between Christ and conscience in three ways: (1) the protesting conscience has not yet been fully conformed to Christ, to whom it needs to give a more full obedience; (2) struggle between Christ and conscience is inevitable because of our imperfect natures, so we need patience to endure unavoidable dark nights of the soul; (3) in spite of Revelation, we have not yet understood the fullness of the Christ who has been sent to us, so we need enlightenment by the Spirit and by study.

These three complementary attitudes toward struggle between Christ and conscience have in common a morality of acquiescence before the authority of Christ past. The Christ who is believed to live eternally "at the right hand of God" is held to be the same as he who took the form of the Nazarene once upon a time. Therefore, the good of humanity must be reliance upon him, and him alone. Whatever is true in the whole of creation and history is *already* true in him. Therefore, any conflict between him and one's conscience must be due to an imperfection in the conscience, in the understanding mind, or in both. It cannot be that the sheep should tell the shepherd which way to go.

To this I feel I must ask, in all seriousness, why not? First, what understanding is at work here concerning the fundamental relation between the redeemer Christ and those who are being redeemed? Is it, all said and done, to have been a one-way relationship? Doctrines of grace, both Protestant and Catholic, have said so; yet I find myself believing that this view is no longer compatible with our salvation.

Second, it seems to me, the history of the church is one in which the sheep *do* from time to time tell the shepherd the direction to go. Looked at plainly, without mystique, Christians have carried Christ hither and yon. They took him from Jerusalem to Athens, from the catacombs to the throne of empire, from civilization to wilderness and back again, from the Old World to the New, from monarchies to democracies, from peace to war, from plantation houses to slave quarters, and recently to the moon. Surely it would be very bad faith to maintain that in all this Christians have simply been sheep following a shepherd. On the contrary, they are *people* doing the best (and sometimes the worst) that they know how to do.

The story of the Christian religion is one of enormous human initiative and of dramatic changes in ethics. It is the story of a wide diversity of peoples who, although they held the name of Jesus in common, adapted their beliefs and practices to quite radical changes occurring in their historical circumstances. It is a fundamental error, and a costly one, for theology to seek the truth of God and the truth of Christianity exclusively in Christ past, to the neglect of the truth involved in Christians' encounters with their changing environments. This is a prevalent error, to be found even in so open-minded a theologian as Hans Küng. Reflecting on the diversity of Christian history, he writes:

> Again, it is not surprising that people ask what really holds the very oddly contrasting twenty centuries of Christian history and tradition together. And again there is no other answer than this: it is the memory of the one Jesus, called also throughout the centuries "Christ," God's last and decisive ambassador. (Küng 1976, p. 122)

This is grand overstatement, typical of christology and ultimately ⌣

crippling to both reason and faith. The "memory of the one Jesus" is as divisive as it is unifying; and the continuity of Christian history, such as it may be, is better ascribed to God than to Jesus.

One of the major moves Christians made in the early centuries was to change the paradigm for envisioning their relation to Christ. This change was an adaptation to historical events, or rather to the lack of an event expected—the return of Christ in glory.

The Christian message had spread rapidly, making converts in many parts of the empire. It spread so fast, among people so radically disaffected from Roman society, that it became the object of persecution. Because of the persecutions, also because time was passing and the church expanding, Christians faced something for which the example and teaching of Jesus had not prepared them: the question of survival. Like it or not, the church could not survive unless it came to terms with social organization and structure, both in the world at large and also within the Christian community. What we know and recognize today as "church" began then to take shape. It began to prepare itself (unwittingly no doubt) for that moment in the fourth century when it would become the established religion, the preservator of a troubled empire and its political structure.

As survival became, step by step, a question of urgency for the fledgling church, as the liberation in the *eschaton* receded toward the far horizon, the paradigm for the interpretation of Jesus was transformed. The sheep did tell the shepherd which way to go. If they had not, there would soon have been no sheep. Without sheep, no shepherd. The church took Christ under its care, to assure his survival. It is perhaps offensive to state matters in this way, but I desire that the church should take responsibility for its own history, its own actions, and not hide behind the rationalization that it has merely tried to follow Jesus. I am not saying the church had a bad motive. The will to survive is not in itself evil, and I am quite ready to see in the survival strategies of the church from the second century onward something of value in the providence of God. The agency of this work, however, was human thought and action. One of its effects was to move Christ from the front of history to its center, from the lead edge of things to their established middle.

The shepherd became surrounded by the sheep. Instead of looking where they were going, the sheep looked inward at their own numbers and at the shepherd in their midst to see where they already were.

In the strict sense of the term, "christology" originated at the same time as the paradigm-shift I am describing. Christology refers to a systematic or carefully reasoned doctrine about who Christ is. Until the church's survival became urgent, requiring persistent attention and discussion, theology remained rather unsystematic. Certainly it made no careful use of philosophical concepts. Earlier, christologies were so unsystematic that they scarcely deserved the name. That is why I stress the eschatological context pervading most of the New Testament: it provides our best clue to the most widespread paradigm for interpreting Jesus in the beginning.

The paradigm-shift was anticipated in some parts of the New Testament itself, notably in the Fourth Gospel:

> . . . the Synoptic idea of the Kingdom of God disappears, and in place of it we have the message of "eternal life." . . . It had always been the Christian belief that the Lord had departed in order to return, not in weakness as he had come at first, but in his Messianic glory. More than two generations had now gone by and there was still no sign of that glorious advent, and many had begun to fear that the hope was in vain. In several of the later New Testament books there is an effort to convince the doubters that, in spite of the long delay, the Lord's promise will presently be fulfilled. The Fourth Evangelist adopts a different method. He declares that Christ has already returned, not in visible form on the clouds of heaven, but as an inward presence in the hearts of his people. (Scott 1932, pp. 254–255)

The Fourth Gospel seems to have been written at or near the turn of the century, 100 C.E. By then, persecutions had begun. In John, the accent falls upon loving participation in Jesus the shepherd, who is also the vine uniting the branches and (in the Prologue) the Word and the light of God that has come into the very midst of a darkened world. Mixing metaphors, the Prologue says that this illumination has "encamped" among us, assuming human form. The literary structure of the Fourth Gospel, utterly unlike the looser synoptic chronicles, reinforces the thought of Christ as center. Its highly formal reduplications, parallelisms, and analogies are so arranged as to suggest concentric circles of events and meanings around the death and resurrection of Jesus. And it is in John that we hear Jesus speak in the perfect tense: "I *have* overcome the world" (John 16:33). In such phrases throughout the Fourth Gospel we may hear the blessed assurance longed for by a threatened community. We know it was threatened from Rome, and this gospel seems haunted by a threat from non-Christian Jews. The Fourth Gospel became the primary New Testament source for Christian mysticism and also Christian anti-Semitism (see Koenig 1979).

We cannot tell how much the author of the Fourth Gospel may have relied on a prevalent context of eschatological expectation for the proper understanding of his gospel. (A clearly eschatological passage at John 5:28–29 seems out of place.) In any case, it is a transitional document between the eschatological messianism of the synoptics and the explicit theologies of Christ the center that emerged later. For these it became, unfortunately, the most important of the New Testament writings.

As the paradigm-shift became more definite, Christ became the center in innumerable respects. The following are among the more salient.

The center or source of creation. The Prologue to the Gospel of John identified Jesus as the *Logos* or creative principle in God. "Without him was not anything made that was made" (John 1:3). In this view Christ does not rescue his people from the structured world. Rather, he is responsible for the creation of all structure from the beginning. The theme is designed to combat all dualisms that might consign the structured world to the Devil, or to the Roman emperor; but the price paid is to identify God with the given structure of the world in a way the Old Testament and the rest of the New Testament had never done. The sensitive ethical issue lies in the confusion the Logos-doctrine engenders between structures of nature and structures of society. If Christ as Logos created "all things," this may be seen to include governmental hierarchies as well as the starry heavens, an interpretation of the matter that was not long in coming.

The center of human being. A controversy in dispute for several centuries (never really laid to rest) concerned the divine and human "natures" of Christ. The balance sought could be maintained only by the kind of paradoxical language adopted at the Council of Chalcedon in 451 C.E.:

> . . . in two natures, without confusion, without change, without division, without separation, the distinction of natures being in no way annulled by the union. . . . (Bettenson 1947, p. 73)

Sometimes the balance tilted toward the side of divinity, sometimes toward humanity. When we read the history of the controversies and see how passionately the theologians sought an equilibrium between human and divine, we discern that the object of the pursuit was to find the exact center of human being, where finite and infinite could meet. If it could be stated (contrary to the assumptions of both Hellenism and Judaism) that Christ was fully human *and* truly divine, then he would be located at the authentic center of creaturehood. He would be perfect.

The center of history. This center follows logically upon the previous one, although concern about it, if Oscar Cullmann (1950) and others are right, began rather early. Two complementary logics led to the same conclusion: (*a*) If all humanity has in principle the same relation to Christ, this must be true in the past and future as well as the present. Equidistant from all times, Christ is their center. (*b*) As bringer of the *eschaton*, Christ is the "end" of history. Yet he has no place there unless he is also its beginning. (Note the quasi-Platonic, classicistic assumption at work: Nothing can be fundamentally new; whatever truly is, or shall be, always was.) His earthly life in Palestine is therefore his appearance in the midst of what he began and will one day end. He is the center of history, who has fulfilled one set of promises (those in the Old Covenant) and given us now another set, which he will again fulfill.

The center of the church. This is perhaps obvious, but it must be mentioned for two reasons: (*a*) However familiar to us, the *centrality* of Christ in the church is not a necessary understanding. In fact, it is challenged every time a committed group of Christ's faithful declare that they are going to *follow* him (like the disciples of old) *away* from present practice. One may follow a leader, but not a center. (*b*) As the center of the church, Christ became a sacramental figure. The church became sacerdotal, and its "ministers" became "priests." Christ became the mediator, whose grace was in turn mediated by a sacramental church.

After the adoption of Christianity by the empire under Constantine, Christ became *the center of society*. It does not appear that he has been very comfortable there, certainly not always welcome. His relation to society has been thrown up in the air in modern times, and christological controversy today has to do with where the church expects "him" to come down.

The christology of Christ the center remains strong today, at least in theory. I cite Hans Küng again, because he is a Catholic theologian embattled against the claims of central authority exercised by Rome. Küng does what Luther did: He tries to free himself from the constricting authority of one center by appealing to another. He appeals to Jesus Christ, the subject of Küng's massive book, *On Being a Christian*. This is entirely understandable, but the Christ to whom he appeals is that one in the center of all things who has precipitated that very crisis of conscience which has brought Rome and Küng to their disagreement. Küng repeatedly refers to Jesus Christ as "ultimate," meaning decisive and final. He calls him "God's last and decisive ambassador" (see above, p. 47) and refers to him repeatedly as "archetype." Insofar as Christ is an archetype, he is of no help to Küng in his dispute with the Vatican. After all, Rome sees *itself* as archetypal and can plausibly maintain that from its central position it can most legitimately interpret the archetypally central Christ. As long as Christ is center, bishops and Holy Sees are automatically authenticated. It is not hard for them to dismiss even a very popular and respected theologian like Küng for being "off center." Indeed he is. And so is Christ; but this, alas, is not noticed.

Appeals to Christ as center, model, and norm are by no means confined to the Roman Catholic church. I cite from an otherwise excellent article on "Homosexuality and the Church," by James B. Nelson, a Protestant. The author states his interpretive principles:

> My first hermeneutical assumption — and the most fundamental one — is that Jesus Christ is the bearer of God's invitation to human

wholeness and is the focal point of God's humanizing action; hence, Jesus Christ is the central norm through which and by which all else must be judged. Second, I believe that the interpreter must take seriously both the historical context of the biblical writer and the present cultural situation. Third, we should study the Bible, aware of the cultural relativity through which we perceive and experience Christian existence. And, fourth, our scriptural interpretation should exhibit openness to God's truth that may be revealed through other disciplines of human inquiry. . . . (Nelson 1977, p. 64, emphasis added)

The principle stating that Jesus Christ is "the focal point" and "the central norm," has no substance. I do not mean that Jesus Christ has not entered into the author's thought, nor influenced the wise ethical position he takes. I mean that the way in which Christ has affected him and informed his judgment is manifestly *not* as central norm but as something else, less clear and less normative. Lip service to Christ as norm has become the rhetoric by which liberals and conservatives alike try to justify their thought as Christian — especially, it seems, when what they propose has scant basis in the gospel accounts of Jesus. Nelson ends up, as I once did (Driver 1965; cf. Chapter 7 below), in an argument from silence. The most that can be said about Jesus and homosexuality is that he said nothing about it! Such lack of evidence can hardly provide a "central norm." Furthermore, this is the situation regarding most of the important ethical decisions we have to make.

The trouble afflicting christological ethics can be revealed by asking what Nelson's first assumption has to do with his second, third, and fourth — or they with it. The second counsels serious attention to historical contexts, both ours and that of the biblical writer. The third, a corollary, refers to "cultural relativity." The last speaks of openness to truth from nontheological sources. We have, then, one central norm and three expressions of relativity. In what way are these relativities connected to the "central norm"? Does it govern their use? If so, how? Do they help one to understand the central norm? If so, how? The author does not say. In fact, he cannot say, for his fixed norm and his assumptions of relativity are incompatible. The same problem occurs throughout modern theology, both liberal and conservative.

A modern understanding of history has no place for a "central norm." To think historically, in the modern sense, is to give up centers and abiding norms. It is to enter wholeheartedly upon the seas of relativity, where all things change, some faster than others. If one takes historical contexts seriously, no historical event may claim to be central to all others.

Christianity has long claimed that the case of Jesus is different. He is supposed to have been *in* the world but not *of* it, in time but not temporal, in history yet above it. Such thoughts were intelligible in past ages, before the idea of history had been radicalized. They are valid no longer.

Curiously, modern historicism is closer to biblical thought than to classical theology. For the most part, the Bible is not concerned with a center or a "central norm." Except for the Johannine litera-ture, this is as true of the New Testament as the Old. Biblical con-cern is with God's activity for justice — present-future and past. This divine activity may be said to be persistent in the Bible, but it is not a historical *center*. It is a motive, not a *fait accompli*. If we say that Jesus is the central ethical norm, we say that the principle of every-thing good has already been revealed in him, since a center stands for the whole. But in fact the example and the teaching of Jesus do not resolve the ethical dilemmas people face. There are several rea-sons for this, an important one being the New Testament eschatology. As it suspended concern for social structures, early Christian eschatology also suspended reflection on the norms and other structures of ethics. When in time the need for norms arose, it was not Christ who provided them but something more subtle, dynamic, and (in the true sense of the word) spiritual. It was the en-counter and interaction among experience, reason, conscience, and Christ. To this encounter Christ came not as norm but as partici-pant in dialogue. If we do not see this, we are not able to interpret and respect the vastly different ethical positions taken by Christians at different times and places.

I feel driven to say that in order to be faithful to Jesus one must refuse him as model or central norm. He himself seems not to have needed a center of history. What he relied on was the power of a loving God. To be sure, that got him crucified; but if Easter means anything, it means the cross did not end nor arrest the power of

God. It need not mean that the love of God is focused forever on Jesus. To say so is to prescind from history and from the ethical decisions that are uniquely ours, having to do with matters that never occurred to Jesus.

We have to face two problems. First, the thought of Jesus Christ as the center of all things, including history, must become a burden intolerable to conscience when one's sense of history becomes what it is in our age. Given modern ideas of history, a "center" (already an alien concept) in the first century becomes ever more distant from us. To look at it, we have to look *backward*. That might perhaps be dignified as remembrance of history, if that "center" did not also mean norm.

Before the modern period, when "history" became linear development, one could look at a center of history without turning backward, for the existence of a "center of history" made the passage of time essentially irrelevant. In classical and medieval thought, from which the idea of a center of time is borrowed, history brought forth nothing new. Under slightly different guises the same things were thought to happen over and over. Their moral significance therefore came from a "center" around which they revolved like the sun around the earth. Today, an ancient event lies "in the dark backward and abysm of time" (*The Tempest*, I. ii. 50). Into that abyss Jesus is receding.

A second problem is that insofar as Jesus is thought to be archetype, norm, or model of human being, or insofar as he is held to be the center of all value, Christian ethics is crippled. The model is insufficient. Most of the New Testament writings were never intended to provide a model, because the writers assumed that the abiding structures and norms of this world were passing away. As one does not write systems for a world about to be desystematized, so one does not sketch models for beings who are on the verge of transposition into a spiritual realm.

The New Testament Christ is Christ future. The message preached by Jesus was the kingdom of God future. In both cases, future meant something God would do pretty soon. What are we to make of this twenty centuries later? How might we get Christ and God out from behind us in the past and around into our present-future without simply using them as symbols for utopia? Could we be true Christians without Christ at our back? Could we, like the Jews, look for a Messiah yet to come, a Messiah who is not necessarily Jesus of Nazareth? Would we still be Christians? That is the question I raise.

I raise it as a christological question: "Who do you say that I am?" (Matt. 16:15). And my motive is ethical: What shall we do in collaboration with God to save human life? When the rich younger ruler asked what he should do to be saved, he received an ethical reply, not words about faith in a central norm (Matt. 19:16–22; Luke 18:18–23; cf. Luke 10:25–37).

Jesus preached a radical turning to God, a plunge forward into *communitas*. He did not, except as depicted in the Fourth Gospel, preach his own centrality and eternity. The churches, however, have taught that Christ is an entirely unique event in history that has occurred once for the salvation of all and once for all time.

To think of Christ as the center, model, and norm of humanity made a certain sense in the Ptolemaic universe, which had the earth as its center. It continued to make some sense, however strained, in the Copernican universe, which had the sun as its center. Today, christocentrism cannot make sense in the Einsteinian universe, which has *no center* and in which every structure is a dynamic relationality of *moving* components.

The churches made their reluctant peace with the Copernican revolution. They have scarcely begun to think about the Einsteinian age of relativity. The ethical theological task of the churches today is to find a christology that can be liberating in a world of relativity.

·4·

Critique of Christ as Once for All

I recall from earlier years a theologian's blackboard diagram:

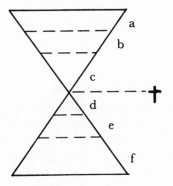

This hour-glass figure was supposed to represent the position of Christ in the history of salvation. Portion *a* stood for the whole of the human race. The smaller portion *b* was the covenanted people of Israel, reduced later to *c*, a "remnant" faithful to the covenant. Then the history passed through the narrow neck of the funnel, which represented Christ Jesus, the incarnate Son of God in whom the covenant was renewed so that it might expand again, first into *d*, the disciples and other early Christians, then into *e*, the ever-expanding church, and ultimately to *f*, the whole of the human race. The diagram expressed so clearly the idea of Christianity I had received as a child that I have never forgotten it. At the time, I did not see anything wrong with it. Today, I am appalled.

I notice today that the Jews disappear from the story once Christ Jesus arrives. They have been supplanted by a "new Israel," the Christian church. Their disappearance belongs to what I called, in Chapter 2, Christianity's latent doctrine of the nonperson.

Theologians also speak of a "scandal of particularity," in the Christian religion. It means the intellectual difficulty involved in believing that the salvation of all has come by way of one particular man, Jesus; but this scandal is not only intellectual. It has become a moral scandal. I do not know whether this was always the case.

I focus my concern on what certain teachings about Christ have become, the effect they have on Christians and non-Christians in our time. From this vantage point I can observe that the immoral factor in the "scandal of particularity" today is its insistence upon a once-for-all Christ in a relativistic world. That is indeed a scandal — erroneous, imperial, and dangerous to humanity. It precludes Christianity's ability to affirm that all people have a right to their place in the sun. It is not meant to do this, but it does. I shall return to the question of relativism shortly.

The Jews are not the only people who disappear from the Christian story as it is usually told. All non-Christian cultures and religions similarly vanish. When they do not, they are seen, as the Jews of Europe once were, only as potential objects of conversion; for the Christian hope, as it has turned out, is that "at the name of Jesus every knee shall bow." In that dream, the cultural diversity of the world is rendered of little account. At best it simply adds texture and color to the one throng gathered around one and the same throne.

After I had spoken in a church on some topic or other, a listener said, "You really do like pluralism, don't you? I mean, it turns you on." I replied that my liking it had to do with my believing in it very deeply. She remarked, "I don't think I have ever before heard a preacher who did." I do not regard myself as unique among preachers in my love of pluralism; but I do think we lack theological, and especially christological, endorsement of this love. The question is how to be a Christian without being paternalistic of those who are not. (I skip over the danger of being openly hostile.)

It is not enough to know and say that "Christ loves everybody." What is at issue is the manner of this love and what it makes of the fact of human diversity.

The diagram opening this chapter put Christ at the center of the human race and at the center of history, ideas which I criticized in the previous chapter. Here I continue that critique with special attention to the idea that Jesus Christ is a saving revelation of God that may occur once only: once for all time and once for all people. I believe we cannot come to a genuine theological appreciation of pluralism and relativity until we have disposed of the notion that there is only one Christ for all time.

In *Patterns of Grace* (pp. 165f.) I wrote that to speak of Christ as "once for all" is to engage in hyperbole. It is testimony, I said, to "God's infinite commitment to finitude."

The context for my remark was a discussion of God as both finite and infinite. However we may understand the doctrine of God's incarnation in Jesus, it surely means that God has been manifest in human form without ceasing to be God. The man Jesus was not a mere mask or costume of God put on for a particular occasion and later taken off. Jesus is not a mere form waiting now in some celestial robing room until God shall put it on again at the end of time for a Second Coming. Ideas of that kind have little to do with Incarnation, and the churches early along rejected them as Docetic, a word which means "in appearance only," not the real thing. As it wrestled with what came to be known as the "two natures" of Christ, the church officially excluded the idea that the savior Jesus was God in reality while human only by appearance. It rejected also the opposite idea, that Jesus was in reality a man who merely *represented* God in some way. The church insisted that Christ Jesus was both divine and human. This classical affirmation (more or less definitive since the Council of Chalcedon in 451 C.E.) is what gave rise to my saying that the revelation in Christ is testimony to "God's infinite commitment to finitude." In Jesus we Christians find a commitment of God to the human condition without reserve. This may be seen as the complement of Jesus' unreserved commitment to God. In Jesus we discern a convergence to the point of identity between what is human and what is divine. On this belief the Christian religion is based, and I am not of a mind to put it aside. I believe, however, that it properly leads to conclusions far different from those commonly reached.

As I look at the suffering world today, at the role the far-flung churches play within it, and at my own stumbling life, I come to think that the churches' big mistake has been to *imprison* God in the likeness of Jesus. Something done for our freedom has been turned into a mold in which we try to hold God fixed. Since God cannot be contained, we encapture only ourselves.

The error is easy to state and hard to undo. The mistake was to have concluded (or insisted) that an infinite commitment of God to human finitude can occur once and once only.

Hellenistic philosophy was quite convinced that God, being perfect, did not change, or move, or even cause movement. As Philo Judaeus put it early in the first century C.E., "There is only one thing that neither *causes* motion nor *experiences* it: our original ruler" (*On the Creation of the World according to Moses; and the Allegory of the Laws, Book I*. Loeb Classical Library, p. 81). Upon such a doctrine of God as that, the Incarnation must appear as something that does not belong in time at all. This idea lingers among us, posing the question how to envision both God and Christ in relation to the motions of history.

If the incarnation of God in finite humanity can occur but once, the religious value of all other human history is nil. This was not a problem for most of the writers of the New Testament, since they believed that the known world was about to come to its end. Even when, as in the case of Paul, they began to wonder if this was so, their thought about the human story was still dominated by a vision of its end. The New Testament's purpose on the whole is to offer, through Christ Jesus, salvation from a doomed world.

In the next four centuries, the eschatological character of early Christianity was shifted toward the christocentrism I have described earlier. With heavy reliance on the gospel of John and corresponding neglect of the synoptics, Christ was interpreted as the eternal center of all creation, including nature, history, church, and temporal government. If the church and the empire did any wrong, it was because they veered from their ideal center in Christ, behaving like a wheel out of balance. When the Roman Empire began to fall, the great theologian Augustine had to acknowledge that the wheel of civilization was badly out of balance and was likely, as such wheels do, to get worse. He therefore devised a theology of two wheels with two different axes or, in his own terms, two cities with different loyalties and principles. This he set forth in *The City of God* (around 412 C.E.), which proposed that a heavenly city exists alongside an earthly one. A faithful Christian is citizen of both, rendering unto God the things that are God's and to the state the things that make for law and order. The Middle Ages saw increasing conflict between the Vicar of Christ as center and feudal king as center. In this contest, the kings learned much from Rome. As has often been observed, the monarchies that emerged in Europe modeled much of their statecraft on the papacy. However, as long as the issues were posed in terms of the centrality of power and authority, the religious value of history did not become a severe question, for if you believe that history is revolving *around* something, you do not find its meaning to be much of a problem. The more it changes, the more it remains the same.

Only with the gradual rise of a post-medieval historical sensibility, which has resulted in an intellectual paradigm-shift in the nineteenth and twentieth centuries, has the religious value of history become an acute problem for Christianity, challenging old ideas of finite and infinite on which the major doctrines of Christ have for so long been based. The reasons for the rise of this historical sensibility are many, but one of the strongest is the dramatic series of changes in socioeconomic and political structure that have occurred in modern capitalism, beginning with the rapid rise of a merchant class in the sixteenth century. It soon became obvious that societies do in time change their structure, not simply by shifting from one king to another, one dynasty to another, or one empire to another, but by change in the very principles of their organization. This means that what we have to come to terms with, as modern people are only too aware, is not only governmental change and the evolution of technologies but structural changes of identity.

It is important to understand what kinds of change and diversity are pertinent here. Certain types of changing are not to my point. Among them are changes belonging to a "cycle of life" and changes of "fortune." The change of an acorn into an oak tree or a youth into an adult are "life-cycle" changes. We do not imagine them to change the identity of the organism, which persists throughout a succession of stages. So also, if I lose all my money and my health, like Job, I have suffered a change in the wheel of fortune but not a change of identity. The kind of change that has become important and troubling for modern thought is structural change amounting to a change of identity. An example is the transformation of a feudal society into a mercantile one, or an agrarian society into an industrial. The world was shocked by Charles Darwin's discovery that apes might turn into human beings in the course of time, and it was shocked again when Einstein figured out that matter might be converted to energy. The changes that challenge our teachings about Christ are the restructuring of cultural life into new forms, such that our very categories of understanding shift. I refer to this kind of change as *historical, cultural,* and *structural.* To speak of change as historical emphasizes the role of time, while to speak of it as cultural highlights the diversity of human life from group to group. Both refer to structural changes in the way life is lived and thoughts are thought.

We are aware today that very significant structural change, manifest in style, values, morals, and basic mental concepts can occur in one generation. Such changes were, of course, noticed also in past ages, even if the changes came slower then. What is new to the theology of the last two centuries is the thought that structural changes in history and nature may have positive religious meaning: the relativity of temporal existence may be part of the creating and redeeming work of God. This thought has come to be widely shared among theologians and in a great deal of preaching. However, it loses much of its force because the christological implication is not carried through: if the relativities of history are to acquire a positive rather than a negative value, Christ cannot remain "central" or "once for all." Christ must be re-conceived in relativistic terms. For this, I have noted earlier, we require a christological paradigm-shift as great as that in the early church when the thought of history's immediate end gave way to the idea of Christ as the center of history's slowly turning wheel.

It was Hegel (1770-1831), standing on the shoulders of Vico (1668-1744) and Joachim of Floris (c. 1132-1202), who realized that a positive philosophical and religious understanding of historical change required a logic different from that of the classical tradition. Classical logic was designed for thinking about truth as timeless. It dealt with temporal phenomena by abstracting from them concepts in which time played no part. It dealt with change by noting similarity and difference, not by valuing the process of change itself.

Modalities of historical change occupied Hegel's mind as much as the position of the earth relative to the sun had earlier occupied the mind of Galileo. Hegel set out to articulate a "dialectical" logic which would be appropriate for an intellectual grasp of history. This logic starts from the assumption that change is not accidental to reality but fundamental. The case is not that things *have* some kind of reality which *happens* to undergo change. Rather, the case is that things are real by virtue of their changing, which is another way of saying that they *are* because they *live* and *become*. The principal category of understanding is thus not permanence but life, and life may be seen to proceed by the generation of antinomies and their subsequent resolution into genuinely new configurations. On this model history comes to be viewed not as a series of ups and downs that have merely secondary interest but as the life of the living world. Hegel's theology proposes that the life of the world and the life of God are two sides of the same life.

I do not subscribe to Hegel's main uses of his own logic. As he proceeded, he came to equate the life of the world with the life of *Geist*, which can be translated as either spirit or mind. Hegel's absorption with Spirit had the unfortunate effect of reducing the history of the world to the history of ideas. Hegel also leapt to the unfortunate conclusion that the acme of world history was reached in Prussian Germany. The idealistic and nationalistic side of Hegel is not my concern, but rather his vitalistic appreciation of history and the logic he propounded to interpret it.

In the dialectical logic of Hegel, the conjunction of finite and infinite is not a paradox. Instead, it is an antinomy which drives toward resolution in ever new configurations. When we experience in ourselves and in our regard of what is good in the world a tension between finitude and infinity (Hegel said concrete and universal), we are experiencing the creativity of God. We are in touch with the ideal not as the memory of something already once given but as the goal which offers value and direction to present existence. The path to this goal must include, not repudiate or discount, everything that opposes it.

Using Hegel's dialectical logic, we may see what now appears as an error of classical thought concerning Christ. The conjunction of finitude and infinity in Jesus was not a logical contradiction. On the contrary, infinity is an aspect of every finite occurrence, and finitude is the dialectical complement of infinity. Moreover, infinity should not suggest permanence or changelessness. Infinity is not a state nor a substance of any kind. It is a quality *of* the finite, the quality of its reach beyond itself toward a completion it does not possess but of which it speaks by its very existence. Without the finite, infinity makes no sense. And if the quality of infinitude were to cease, all things finite would disappear. Losing their horizon of meaning, they would fade from view.

"Dialectical reciprocity of finite and infinite" is philosophical language for what religions know as the presence of the divine in the here and now. The study of world religions informs us that virtually any finite thing or person may become the occasion of divine presence. "The gods," Euripides was fond of saying, "have many shapes." Similar testimony comes from the "varieties of religious experience" in our own Western culture (James 1902; E. Robinson 1977).

Christianity in the West (less clearly so in the East) has tried to sever the inherent connection between finite and infinite, partly in order to insist on the absolute transcendence of God (therefore "his" difference from all other, "false" gods) and partly in order to say that God's incarnation in Jesus was a unique, miraculous gift of God's grace. In Western Christian theology, therefore, the infinity of God has often been regarded as the divine essence, prior to and alien from the finite created world. That this is both a philosophical and a religious error was maintained by Friedrich Schelling in *The Ages of the World*, a work begun in 1811:

Since God in himself neither is nor is not, and also cannot come to be by a movement in himself . . . so he cannot anywhere be or come to be (in an eternal way) in himself, but only in relation to something else [Schelling 1942, pp. 144f.].

We know of no other than a living God; that connection of his highest spiritual life with a natural one is the original secret of his individuality, the miracle of indissoluble life . . . [p. 147].

In other words, infinity makes sense and is godly only in relation to finitude. Beyond that, as I have argued elsewhere, the attempt to value the infinite more than the finite, and to deny that God is both, results in an evil degradation of finite life (Driver 1977, pp. 152–161). Here I may add that to regard the incarnation of infinite God in finite Jesus as paradoxical, unprecedented, and "final" also results in evil. It leads to the degradation of other religions and indeed of all experience that is not identifiably "Christian." That text in the Fourth Gospel which makes Jesus to say, "No one comes to the Father except by me" (John 14:6) should be repudiated, along with the rest of that gospel's elitist, christocentric anti-Semitism.

To see Jesus as a conjunction of finite and infinite is to see him neither as unique in all time nor as changeless. Instead of thinking that there is some timeless quality in Jesus which abides after we have discounted everything that has to do with his historical particularity (his Jewishness, his bachelorhood, his poverty, his vocation as a wandering teacher, his ancient world-view, his masculinity, his obsession with the end of the age, his speaking the Aramaic language, etc.), we should insist on that historical particularity as the sign of his *changing* infinity. In other words, the infinite commitment of God to finitude in Jesus does not indicate something done once and once only for all time. It speaks of a God of life committed without reserve to the finitude of life in historical time. Infinity is what saves finite things both from death by dissolution and from death by permanence. Infinity is the dynamic of existence — in biblical language, the "spirit of life."

The infinity of Christ Jesus is the moral dynamic in him which awakens us to value his finitude and which also forbids us to circle around him forever. To value that finite life, to prize, hold dear, and rejoice in that God-obsessed, itinerant, ascetic, male, wonder-working, Jewish, apocalyptic, crucified, resurrected, big-hearted, deep-suffering wayfarer born in an age remote from us now is to break free of trying to model ourselves upon him. As he had his finitude, so we have ours. They are not the same. If we betray our own destiny in the vain thought that his was better, we are lost indeed. This is the lesson I draw from the doctrine of Incarnation.

They called him Emmanuel: "God with us." To be *with* is to belong to the same relational field and to undergo change alongside one's companion. My friend remains my friend over long years by ceasing to be what she was. Otherwise, when we meet again after I have aged, we could not know each other. Fidelity is the very opposite of unchanging. If God in Christ had done something "once for all," that would be a betrayal of us who move in time. I have no need of a time-stopping savior who would rescue me from the flux of finitude. Finitude is not my problem, nor any part of my sin. My problem is to have betrayed my brothers and sisters.

I must amplify the allusions I have made to relativity. I am gradually becoming convinced that the gap between Christianity and modern theories of relativity is widening so much that the churches' teaching about Christ is in danger of losing both its intellectual and its moral credibility. Christianity has already become socially reactionary in most quarters and will surely become more so as long as its christology opposes those concepts of relativity which have transformed not only the natural and the social sciences but also many ordinary assumptions about the world. The task, then, is to understand what relativity means and how God, Christ, and the world may be understood in its terms.

Relativity is a theoretical concept designed for understanding the fact of pluralism. Its opposite may be called absolutism, monism, or idealism, all of which attempt to reduce any pluralism to a single principle or idea. Instead of seeking to reduce the many to the one, relativity focuses on the forms of relation between phenomena. By pluralism, I do not mean merely a multiplicity of existing things. I mean a multiplicity of *systems* of organization, understanding, and power, each system having a certain legitimate autonomy. Human languages provide a clear example of pluralism in this sense. The fact that translation from one language to another is possible shows that languages can be understood in relation to each other, while the fact that no translation is truly adequate to the original utterance shows that the plurality of languages is every bit as real as any factor they have in common. If the linguistic theory of Noam Chomsky concerning a universal "deep structure" of grammar is taken as a way of reducing all languages to various modes of articulating one and the same set of basic grammatical structures, it flies in the face of pluralism and is probably false. Taken as a postulate concerning the potential relatedness of languages, it is useful. Instead of assuming that unity is prior to diversity, relativity understands unity as a creative process engendered by the prior existence of plurality. Moreover, it differs from both classical and modern process philosophy (Whitehead 1929) by abandoning the notion of a prior ontological ground for the unitive process. Relating, so to speak, is its own ground. It is not made possible by anything un-relational that is prior to it, whether this be called the One, or the First Cause, or Essential Being, or God Alone, or the Primordial Nature of God, or whatever. Relativity concerns itself with the emergent relations between systems (entities) that are genuinely different. To preserve that genuineness, it deals with relations of a *mutual* character, not those which would subsume one system under another. Relativity is therefore mysterious and even frightening to persons who do not believe that the difference between systems is itself good, perhaps the source of all other goodness.

The spread of relativity theory in the modern world is in itself a new phenomenon, at least in Western civilization. By and large the churches have resisted it, often because many persons confuse theories of relativity with moral relativism, which they regard as a way of rationalizing every sort of belief and behavior. This is not, however, a necessary conclusion to be drawn from relativity theory, which does not content itself with the mere observation of plurality but is concerned with the theoretical and functional consequences of pluralities in relation to each other. Although relativity theory in the realm of morals does inhibit the regard of any one system of values as absolute, it does not on that account conclude they are all the same. It locates the problem of values in the actual and potential relation between different value systems as they impinge on one another, and thus it projects the idea of "the good" forward into the unfinished dynamic of cultural interaction.

Relativity theory is most famous in connection with physics, where it is associated with Albert Einstein's name and is well understood only by specialists, among whom neither I nor most of my readers are numbered. Our daily exposure is not to a plurality of systems of physics but to a plurality of cultures, subcultures, religions, social classes, and political systems. When I think of relativity, I think of its meaning in both physics and the social sciences. That the idea of relativity has come to the fore in both science and culture at the same time is surely no accident.

The growth of modern relativity theory has come about in two major stages, the first of which was long opposed by theology while the second is simply being ignored.

The first stage may be said to have begun with Copernicus. Galileo soon recognized that the Ptolemaic earth-centered model of the heavens and the Copernican sun-centered model constituted two systems of thought and gave rise to two closely connected ideas of relativity. Each of the models was a way of expressing the relation between the earth and the sun. You could, with some justification, say either that the sun's motion was relative to the earth at rest (the Ptolemaic system) or that the earth's motion was relative to the stationary sun (Copernicus). In either case, you had a system of movement relative to stability. It is important to notice that "stability" here has meaning only in relation to the movement of the other body. Moreover, as Galileo saw, the Ptolemaic and the Copernican systems were relative to each other. Information acquired by using one of the models could be translated into the terms of the other, and science could go forward in great strides by doing just that. For example, one could perform an experiment in the framework of the earth-centered system and then transform its quantitative results, using mathematical equations, into the terms of the sun-centered system. Within each system, and again in the mathematical transformation of the one to the other, one would be expressing sets of relations. The important point here is that neither the earth nor the sun was assumed to be *necessarily* at rest. It was a question of (*a*) how one viewed one heavenly body relative to the other, and (*b*) how one viewed each *system* relative to the other. The core idea of relativity is expressed in the prepositional phrase, "relative to."

Galileo's ideas were opposed by the university at Bologna and by the church at Rome. What both objected to was the concept of relativity, for it seemed to, and in fact did, undercut the absolute certainty of knowledge. Gains in theory and in new information were bought at the expense of the absoluteness of any one system of knowing. "The new philosophy," as John Donne soon wrote, "puts all in doubt." It was feared that relativity would lead to total skepticism. Instead, it has led to a vast expansion of knowledge obtained by the application of what has more recently been called a "hermeneutic of suspicion."

The first stage of the era of relativity is associated in natural science with the names of Copernicus, Galileo, and Newton. In the social sciences and philosophy the most important figure was Friedrich Hegel. I have already mentioned Hegel's discovery that classical logic was not suitable for the analysis of historical processes, which led him to propound for this purpose a dialectical logic. The result of this was to relativize historical phenomena, viewing each one relative to its position and function in an overall movement of history, which meant also in relation to its dialectical antithesis at the time of its occurrence. Furthermore, the Hegelian logic itself stood in dialectical relation to classical logic, which it partly subsumed and partly opposed. From one point of view, the older logic was still valid and had to be used even by the dialectician of history. If, however, it was taken as *the* logic of an eternal rational principle, it was a deception issuing in wrong conclusions.

In spite of Hegel's own view of history as the gradual realization of an Absolute, his conceptual apparatus for thinking about history is relativistic. He and other Romantic thinkers in the nineteenth century cleared the path for the development of sociology, anthropology, psychology, and the other natural sciences which operate on the basis of relativity, enabled by it to appreciate the world's diversity of cultural systems and the phenomena of structural change within and among them. In this context, Christianity has been compelled to see itself as a religion *relative to* other religions and *relative to* the history of the world. Even today, however, Christianity does this reluctantly, for its tradition and self-understanding are to claim for Christ a unique and untouchable position in both time and eternity. The principle of relativity in modern thought (like the experience of pluralism in modern life) is openly resisted in some theologies and seen as an acute problem in others. Very seldom is it regarded as an opportunity for Christianity to understand itself better. This failure of nerve causes ever greater difficulty, especially since modern cultures are now moving into a second, more radical stage of relativity.

The second stage is rightly associated with the name of Albert Einstein, but the concept through which he was able to radicalize Galileo's ideas of relativity was developed in the nineteenth century by Michael Faraday, H. R. Hertz, and James Clerk Maxwell. I refer to the scientific concept of a *field* of energy. When Einstein began to think about physics around 1900, mechanical theory as formulated classically by Isaac Newton existed alongside, and in contradiction to, field theory as formulated mathematically by Maxwell. Einstein's life was devoted to overcoming this contradiction, which he did by subsuming the Newtonian mechanical paradigm under a theory of relativity that culminated in a "unified field theory." Einstein's "special theory" of relativity had appeared in 1905, the so-called general theory in 1916, and the unified field theory in 1950.

Since I am concerned with Einstein's ideas only insofar as they affect culture and subsequently theology, I need mention only the concepts that are best known and most consequential for our general views of reality. The essential element of a *field* theory, said Leopold Infeld in *Albert Einstein: His Work and Its Influence on Our World* (1950), "is the description of *changes* that spread continuously through *space* and *time*" (p. 11, author's italics). When one thinks in terms of a field theory, one subordinates the notion of *objects* to the idea of *changing patterns* of energy. Einstein was able to show that objects (masses) *are* energy. The devastating truth of $E = Mc^2$ became a fact of modern life in 1945, one of its results being that the absolute character of any "substance" or any unchanging form has been demolished. Conversely, the idea of radiational energy has become *more* substantial than ever before. Field theories nowadays pertain not only to physics but also to psychology (Gestalt psychology especially), sociology, anthropology, and philosophy.

Before the explosion of the atomic bomb, Einstein's idea of mass relative to energy was not as provocatively famous as that of time relative to space. Both ideas were part of the "special theory" of relativity published in 1905, which evoked from a Polish physicist the exclamation, "A new Copernicus has been born!" (Infeld 1950, p. 44). Einstein's theory not only required imagining time and space relative to each other; it also required conceiving of space-time as relative to velocity. As one approached the speed of light, time would slow down. If one exceeded the speed of light, which Einstein thought impossible, time would run "backward." Such ideas about the relativity of time seem as weird as Einstein's conception of the curvature of space, which belongs to the "general theory." The importance of the latter, for my purpose, is that it reinterpreted the phenomenon of gravity, conceiving it no longer as a "force" operating between bodies of mass but as a field. The presence of masses of energy within the gravitational field warps or "curves" space. In other words, space, time, force, and mass are all reinterpreted under the concept of a dynamic field, which means a pattern of *changing* relationships. These changing relationships are all we have to deal with. The interpretation of data does not assume any fixed point in either space or time.

Einstein's theory did assume one fixed or absolute quantity: the velocity of light. It appears as c in $E = Mc^2$ and figures as an invariant number in all of Einstein's calculations. He supposed that no greater velocity is possible in the universe. Today there is some evidence that it may not be so. Modern scientific theory is compelled to imagine a system in which there are no constant values except those introduced by the observer for purposes of observation and reasoning. This does not mean that there are not "laws," regularities, and knowable structures in nature. Rather, it means that the structures are patterns of changing relatedness, of which there can be no *final* knowledge. Martin Buber's religious idea, "In the beginning is the relation," finds an echo in scientific theory.

The second, Einsteinian stage of relativity theory has been paralleled in the social sciences by so many thinkers that no single name can stand for the whole. Darwin's theory of evolution, along with several other such theories in the nineteenth century, showed that organic forms are slowly changing patterns of relation within an ecological field. Both the parts and the whole of this field change during vast epochs of time because they are composed of forces not in perfect equilibrium. The forms we see in nature have only relative stability, an idea shared also by modern geology and astronomy. Hegel, as I have noted, had a similar idea about human institutions and cultures, and so did Karl Marx, who surpassed Hegel by showing that human systems of thought (ideologies) are relative to the system of production and distribution of goods at any time and to the structures of power which attempt to maintain that system.

Marx's thought opened the way to what may be regarded as the epitome of the second stage of modern relativity theory in the social sciences: the "sociology of knowledge." Inquiries under this name have led to the insight that the very structures of our knowing, beginning with sense perceptions and "commonsense" reality, and going on to include language, concepts, and logic, are relative to the social systems in which they occur. Since social systems are of markedly different character at various times and places, the forms of knowledge they generate are also markedly different. One is driven then to speak of a "social construction of reality," according to which the experience of reality, its appearance, its meaning, and all we may know of it are relative to the cultural matrix in which we have learned how to "know" (see Berger and Luckmann 1966). Where "knowledge" varies, of course, so does value. Conversely, values generated by a social group's need to survive, to exercise some measure of power, and to have a shared understanding of good and bad, go far to determine the structure of knowledge in a given social history. The stability of such structures is also relative. Some are more durable than others, having more internal equilibrium and more resilience in the face of novelty, but none exists without change.

The variety of cultural systems in the world has given rise in the post-Hegelian world to the science of anthropology, not to mention such disciplines as comparative literature, comparative history, and comparative religions (often called history of religions). The questions and problems confronting modern anthropologists are not conceivable apart from our own culture's permeation (in educated circles) by the concept of relativity. In a word, the problem is what to make of the astonishing diversity that is found among human cultures.

Various answers have been given. Early anthropologists, notably Sir James Frazer, compiled available information and interpreted it from the vantage point of their own culture. *The Golden Bough* (1890) is a kind of encyclopedia. A second generation, led perhaps by Bronislaw Malinowski, practiced careful firsthand observation in "the field," turning themselves into "participant observers" so as to learn how an exotic culture looked from the inside, how its beliefs, customs, and institutions were structured as a coherent system, and how the parts and the whole functioned together for the well-being of that system. This method fostered appreciation of cultures as discrete systems, each with its own logic and *raison d'etre*. This simple understanding of relativity — that the elements of any culture are relative to the whole of it — has not been able to avoid a more complex problem in all relativity theory, a problem that is at once intellectual and ethical: namely, how to understand the relations that arise *between* cultures, whether in the course of comparative studies or in the cross-cultural contacts provided by historical events. Indeed, Malinowski's study of the Trobriand Islanders, to take but one example, was itself a historical event occasioned by circumstances he did not plan and having social consequences far beyond any he could have envisioned. The Trobrianders and the Europeans have both been changed by it, as is the case whenever strong contact is made between cultures. This enables us to perceive that anthropology is part of that very relativity which it sets out to study. Participant observation, far from being simply a technique, is the way of all knowledge in one degree or another. The same point was made for the physical sciences by Werner Heisenberg in his "uncertainty principle." That the observer's own cultural matrix biases the observation in certain (often unconscious) ways, and that the observer necessarily intervenes in the process she or he is observing, shows that the condition of relativity has an ethical as well as an intellectual dimension. The very act of study has consequences. It cannot therefore be regarded as leading to "pure" knowledge. In the case of anthropology, it will lead to knowledge relative to the cultural matrix emerging from the contact between the cultures of the observer and the observed.

In the face of so much relativity, some anthropologists have thrown up their hands, lapsing into a view others deride as "mere relativism," which means the opinion that all cultures are of equal value, so that from their differences no conclusions can be drawn. Some other anthropologists have sought a finite number of generalizations applicable to all cultures — the existence everywhere of religion, law, custom, and institutions, for example — out of which to construct a "common humanity." Still others, harking back to the Enlightenment's belief in universal reason as the innate human quality overlaid by cultural diversity, have propounded a "structural" analysis. The latter, much indebted to Claude Lévi-Strauss, is based on the premise that there are certain inherent structures of opposition in human thought. Its analyses seek to reveal those universal structures in every culture. The method leads to a hermeneutic of symbols, mores, myths, and intracultural conflicts. The method is very enlightening in certain respects, but not in others. Its critics have often pointed out that it is unable to deal with processes of social change, since the structures of thought which it postulates are envisioned as timeless or, in its own language, synchronic. An incapacity to value and interpret social change has also been noticed in the earlier structural-functionalist method of Malinowski and others (Jarvie 1964).

The intellectual-ethical problem confronting anthropology today is not likely to find a ready solution, for the discipline is itself a part of that problem, lacking any way to extricate itself. This situation is shared, and known to be shared (this is the important new factor), by all the humanities and even the "hard" sciences today. Our knowledge is relative to our time, place, and sense of motivation in history. In this respect we are not different from whatever it is we would know. Whether we study human beings or physical nature, we study systems of relativity; and the intervention of our knowing adds yet another relative dimension. Wordsworth spoke more than he knew when he said, "I am a part of all that I have known."

―――――――

Returning now to christology, I find it in a position similar to that of anthropology. The churches would like, as they have always done, to claim that Christ is universal. The traditional formula that Christ Jesus is "once for all" has expressed such a universal claim.

We find, however, that we can only make it at the expense of any positive appreciation of cultural diversity and the historical inter-action of religions and cultures.

The belief that Christ is once for all has produced cultural im-perialism in Christian missions, both at home and abroad. It has also led Karl Barth and others to suppose that the revelation of God in Christ has nothing to do with human culture and experience. Barth seems not to have noticed that in that case it has nothing to do with anything whatever, since apart from culture we and our world do not exist.

A Christ once for all would be a Christ abstracted from culture, therefore not at all the Jewish messianic figure depicted in the New Testament. Indeed, such a Christ, not culturally shaped, would not be human. As Clifford Geertz has observed, it is only through the guidance of particular cultures that the human race and its individ-ual members become human (Geertz, 1965). The universality of Christ is not preexistent and already given (*pace* the Gospel of John) but is rather an eschatological expectation. Meanwhile, what we have, thank God, is a plurality of Christs, a number of evolving Christs increasingly engaged in cross-cultural and ecumenical inter-action. We know this to be the historical case, but there is a tend-ency to regard it as a pity. On the contrary, it is the sign of our eventual liberation.

We have reached a stage of history, characterized by awareness of relativity, in which the more we make absolute claims about Christ the more we empty Christ of all meaning. Ideas that do not make sense *within* relational fields make no sense at all, deceptively at-tractive as they may be. We are in danger of losing Christ utterly through our attempts to make Him (*sic*) a fixed and eternal point for all time.

Theology can make no statement about God or Christ which de-scribes what is always the case. Theology may not even postulate a God truly knowable only to "himself." We need to understand that "Christ" is the changing pattern of our relation to a living God. The christological task is to discern the features of this pattern in present-future time, and the only way to do this is to take with radical seriousness our ethical expectations. What we expect (not merely hope) to occur in the ethical life of the world is what informs us about our life relative to God, relative to other people, and relative to what we suppose has happened in the past. The barometer of all christic relatedness is the state of our conscience relative to what is expected in present-future time.

"Transcendence is radical immanence." The sentence is one I wrote in *Patterns of Grace* (p. 164). There it had to do with the doctrine of God. Here I apply it to Jesus. In both cases, it calls for us to discover in our finite here-and-now a vocation of God. What else are we for? The God who calls us is no more outside our history than within it. God is no more in a once-for-all incarnation in Jesus than in our present, fragile moment. For that matter, God is no more tomorrow than today. But God's tomorrow, like our own, is a matter of movement from now to then. The church should teach nothing about Christ which suggests going backward or standing still.

The churches seem to believe that since there was only one Jesus there is only one Christ for all time. The churches say that, in Jesus, God has already done the one thing necessary for our salvation. If we still wait, as we do, for the release of our world and ourselves from suffering, we are said to be waiting for the return of the very same Christ who already came once before in Galilee. If we look for guidance and comfort now, we are told to find it in the memory of the Jesus who is depicted in the New Testament. ("Here, try this remedy: it worked for my grandfather.") In the sacrament of The Lord's Table, we are supposed to perpetuate the single moment in time which has infinite value until the end of time. As there is only one God, so it is thought, there is only one incarnation, one Christ, and one name upon which we may call for our justification in the eyes of God. Under this principle of the simple one-ness of Christ, as my eyes see it, the living God is obscured. It is as if, having noticed and been amazed by God's infinite commitment to finitude in Jesus, we had said, "God be praised! Now we can be sure he won't do *that* again." No? Tell it to the dead in Auschwitz. Tell it to the landless people, unwelcome on any shore, adrift in the South China Sea. Are we to regard the destitute of this earth as unfortunate casualties in a drama that cannot change because God made once and once only an infinite commitment to finitude?

The most familiar reply to questions such as these I raise is to say that the once-for-all revelation of God does not change but that *we* can change. This is what I mean by the imprisonment of God in the likeness of Jesus. Who are we, after all, even if we have been granted the Christian revelation, to say that God may not do whatever God pleases? Who are we to say that God is bound by what God has already done? And by what odd logic do we say this in the name of that very person who reminded us that the Spirit of God changes direction like the wind, no one knowing where it comes from or where it goes (John 3:8)? Much is said these days about the gospel as a message of human liberation, but it is not much noticed that human beings cannot be any more free than is their God. A God conceived as bound to "his" own past, even in the gracious form of Jesus, is in no position to liberate people from bondage to *their* past. To preach that God in Jesus has made the "final revelation" of "himself" is to baptize the status quo to the end of time, for it says that God has already done the best that God can do. In that case, all our best-intentioned social action, our most enlightened revolutionary praxis, is mere tinkering with the situation in which God has left us. And this is, in fact, what most Christians, with fairly good logic, do conclude. For them, as for Augustine in *The City of God*, the earthly political role of the church is to conserve as much good order as possible in a world that will not get any better than it already is. Meanwhile, salvation has to do with a heavenly city, to which some Christians already belong by virtue of their "faith." Here "faith" means not only trust in God but specifically a trust in what God has already done, once for all time.

My reader will have noticed, I trust, my rhetorical use of the word "already." In the name of a present-future Christ, I take arms against the perfect tense: "has done," "has made," "did once," "already accomplished," "made perfect in himself. . . ." I believe we Christians suffer needlessly the burden of a past-perfect perfection. Belief in it blinds us to the present-future work of God. We cannot see the miracles in front of our eyes. We are like the United States Government, which can see in Nicaragua's Sandinista revolution only the loss of the already known Somoza regime or its supplantation by an already known Castroism. The United States does not imagine that the Sandinistas or the revolutionaries in El Salvador may have envisioned something new and good. It will therefore, in all likelihood, force them into a corner and ensure that they can survive only by choosing among the powers that "already" exist. Our faith in what we already know rewards us with repetition of what we have already been through, except that history never does completely repeat itself. What turns up new in history confounds all true believers in the perfect tense, who mostly try to stifle the new.

Ours is a time of history when some old verities are shaken. One of them was given exquisite phrasing by Shakespeare at the time of the Renaissance of classical thought in Europe:

> *love is not love*
> *Which alters when it alteration finds,*
> *Or bends with the remover to remove.*
> *O no, it is an ever-fixed mark*
> *That looks on tempests and is never shaken. . . .*
> (from Sonnet 116)

The words could easily apply to Christ conceived as once-for-all, and with a similar image the prophet Hosea had depicted the constant love of God for a wayward Israel. It is usual among Christians to assume that God "alters not," even though "his" (always "his") people change their ways, ever for the worse. But what if the situation is reversed, as some of the prophets discerned it might be? What if the people are constant while *God* goes off in another direction? Can we imagine ourselves as faithful lovers wondering if we can endure some new adventure of God? A dialogue with a traditional believer might go as follows:

"Oh sure. After all, God is God. His (yes, *his*) ways are mysterious, but he can do no wrong. Stay in church, and he'll come around in time."

"That's not what I'm asking. I'm asking if we can imagine that God might *betray* the church. Might betray Jesus, which means to leave part of himself (yes, *him*self) behind. Might decide to go back to the Jews, join the Marxists, or (what are we coming to?) take up with a witches' coven?"

"This cannot be. The one thing we know about God is that God is faithful. The manifold mystery of God never means that the mind and will of God change. Whatever God does, or doesn't do, he cannot betray his infinite commitment to finitude in Jesus. If you say anything different, *you* have betrayed God."

"I wonder. All the people I have ever loved have changed. And so have I. Love that cannot alter when it finds alteration must itself die, I think. I'd go further: It has to abide *betrayal*. We've always said God's love does that. I'm asking if *our* love of *God* can do it. On the cross, Jesus thought that God had forsaken him. Maybe that was true. Maybe Jesus' love of God was such that it suffered betrayal. Is it possible that we are called to love a God who lets us down? Maybe our love of an unfaithful God is the best thing about us, our deepest human quality, our mirror *imago dei*? God and humanity: lost lovers, betraying each other."

"Your heresy leaves me speechless."

"If this is what it's about, if this is the story, then the ethic is clear: do not attempt to save yourself, and do not attempt to save God: feed the children. In this sense, the Roman Catholic church has been right all along: what matters in love is not the lovers but their progeny. It doesn't matter whether I am happy, now or in the life to come. It doesn't matter whether God is good, faithful, and true. what matters is whether my relation to God feeds the hungry."

"The poor we shall always have with us."

"Which is why we cannot get rid of God. It's why God is not dead."

"I think you should take care for the salvation of your soul."

"It will get saved in the feeding of the children or it's not worth saving."

"But what about *their* souls?"

"It is for them to find whom they will feed. As you said, the poor are always with us."

That doesn't sound like christology. Somewhere Jesus got left behind, we went on to God, and finally ended with nothing more than feeding the hungry. (Nothing *more?*) You don't need to be a Christian to feed the hungry. What should the churches teach about Christ?

"Infinite commitment to finitude." The mistake often made is to think that "infinite" entails permanence, eternity. It is true that the word "infinite" means "without end" and that "eternity" denotes the same, while its connotation is "without a temporal ending," "forever." We can see how the thought of Jesus as divine (infinite, eternal) human being (finite, temporal) led to the idea that he should be seen as the timeless moment in time, the one historical event remaining valid forever, the "center" around which everything turns and the "finis" to which everything points. These thoughts all make sense together as long as we are thinking in terms of Euclidian space and chronological time. Euclidian spaces are defined by peripheries, centers, and lines in between. Chronological times have beginnings, endings, and intervals between. In such space or time, one may drop a center point and imagine all else defined by reference to that point. This has been the traditional pattern of christology: place Jesus in the center and work it out from there.

The picture becomes very different, however, if our terms of reference are neither Euclidian nor chronological but moral. If our question is not, "Where shall we imagine our location in the universe?" or "How shall we locate ourselves in time?" but rather, "What shall we do next?" then the christological picture is of a different sort: we do not look for a center point of reference but for *pointers* to the future. We do not confuse the one with the other. I know that in order to get where I am going I need both to remember where I've come from and to move away from it. If I do not break away, I will wander in circles. And if I do not remember where I was, I will again circle back. Inasmuch as my concern is *moral,* I intend to remember the past so that I can head out from it in a good direction. What is morally good is improvisation upon a good theme, and the story of Jesus makes nothing clearer than that this requires not only the honoring but also the *betrayal* of the original, the willingness not to treat it as sacrosanct, even though it has brought one to life. Such is our challenge now with regard to Jesus.

I, white male, man of my time, good in my way, bad in my way, some sort of Christian in the United States of America, twentieth-century resident of New York City, dream the wild dream that I might look Jesus in the eye as does a woman, a black person, or any other soul who cannot find in Jesus the ideal of one's self. If I do not conform to Jesus, what hope is there for me? How is God to express an infinite commitment to *our* finitude?

"Go forward," said Alex Haley's people in *Roots.* If Christians say it, we have to imagine that God and Christ go forward, too. They respect their past, and they go forward to things new. The Christ of faith is not the one we knew yesterday but the one we expect to meet while going forward.

In Wallace Stevens' *Sunday Morning* a woman of our time, alienated from the teachings of the church and separated from Jesus by the "wide water" of centuries, asks a heretical question which eats at the conscience of many Christians these days: "Why should she give her bounty to the dead?" In the poem's last stanza she receives an answer:

> *She hears, upon that water without sound,*
> *A voice that cries, "The tomb in Palestine*
> *Is not the porch of spirits lingering.*
> *It is the grave of Jesus, where he lay."*

Note the poet's careful use of the past tense to vivify the present.

·5·

Critique of Biblicism

In Chapter 3 I argued against the teaching that Christ is the center of life, and in Chapter 4 I took issue with the idea that Christ Jesus was a work of God done once and once only for the whole of history. The aim in both cases has been to liberate Christian thoughts about God from an imprisonment in the likeness of Jesus and to free Christian conscience to address in good faith the relativities of present-future time. My critique of received ideas must go one step further before I turn to the constructive proposals of my concluding three chapters. The present chapter is devoted to a critique of biblicism, for the idea that Christ is the timeless center of life is paralleled and reinforced by the view that the Bible sets the necessary limits to what the church may believe and teach concerning Christ.

I shall write of the Bible as a whole, not merely the New Testament and not merely those passages which scholarship may consider more "authentic" than others in their representation of Jesus' life and teaching. From earliest days, as we can see in the New Testament itself, Christians have regarded the Old Testament as a kind of witness to Christ, much to the consternation of Judaism. The problem of biblical authority is in no way reduced by confining our attention to those parts of the Bible which speak directly of Jesus. Even if we do not consider the Old Testament, and even if we conclude that parts of the New Testament are more reliable than others in what they say of the "historical" Jesus, it is still to the Bible that we are looking, and so the matter of its proper authority for ethical teaching about Christ has not changed. Questions about the relation of the Old Testament to the New and about the historical accuracy of the gospels raise issues of biblical interpretation (hermeneutics) which do not affect the prior question of the Bible's right to be the object of so much attention.

The imprisonment of God in the likeness of Jesus, and for that matter the captivity of Christ in the likeness of Jesus, are both the consequence of the churches' having bound themselves to the texts of scripture. Christians, like Jews, have been defined as a "people of the Book." However good this biblical identity may have been at certain times past, it is not good today, for it does not correspond to the adaptive and creative strategies which are necessary now for the survival of humanity on earth, not to mention the justice we owe to our destitute neighbors on the planet who are at this very time perishing by the millions. No amount of fidelity to the Bible, no amount of reading it, and no excellence in the science or art of its interpretation can (to cite one example) provide either the motive or the know-how to stop the world's population explosion. It cannot (for another) tell us whether we should or should not go on developing nuclear energy. However, the action or inaction of the churches concerning these issues tells much about what Christ they recognize and worship.

The authority of the Bible emerges *within*, and not *prior to*, our experience of the present world and its possible future. The polemic of this chapter therefore is directed not against any biblical authority whatever but against its being "foremost" and unique. As I have already warned against seeing Christ as unique or central, so I argue now against a similar regard of scripture. As Christians, our first concern should be neither Christ nor the Bible but the world of God, the world in ethically creative relation to God's creating. I believe it is possible to show, on the basis of the gospels, that this was Jesus' own concern. However, it should not be ours simply because it was his. We should and do have other reasons as well. The authority of Jesus and of scripture for Christians does not stand by itself: it is one part of the complexity of our ethical life, and the churches would be more credible if they frankly said so. We should not ask what the Bible "tells" us, but how it helps, and also hinders, our collaboration with God. This is the same question we should ask in our recognition of Christ. It is, indeed, the question we should address to every "authority": How are you helping and how are you hindering me and my neighbor to do what we ought to do? Subservience to authority looks only for help. A so-called disrespect for authority sees only hindrance, while the "authority" that is "disrespected" is apt to see only disobedience. A genuine authority acknowledges imperfection, even harm, in itself. A genuine authority can repent of its own error. If the Bible has any right to be authoritative for us, it respects our duty to see wherein it goes wrong, harms us, and hinders our relation to God.

To regard the Bible's authority in mutual relation to my own conscience was but little conveyed to me as a child growing up in southern Protestantism. Nor did the picture change very much when I went north to study at a seminary reputed to be the most liberal in the nation. I saw that my liberal teachers advocated certain ideas and certain social values that Bible Belt conservatives were dead set against, but both sides appealed to "the authority of the Bible." When they fought bitterly, they looked to me like two dogs fighting over the same bone, the Bible. They both "knew" how to read it and therefore had "authority" to reach the "right" conclusions. I agreed with the liberals, but as time went by I came more and more to think that the terms of the argument were spurious. The real argument had to do with goals and values brought *to* the reading of the Bible, not discovered in it as if for the first time. This did not mean the Bible had *no* significance. It meant that the Bible's significance could not be divorced from, nor seen as prior to, the life one was already living and intending to live in the future.

If I first make up my mind how I intend to live and then read the Bible to find support for this, I can attribute to the Bible only an artificial authority. If I think, by contrast, that I first read the Bible and then conclude from it how to live, I have turned it once more into a spurious authority. Genuine authority arises among parties who do not claim priority for themselves, nor ascribe it to each other. Genuine authority, being a kind of love, exists "in between."

In churches and theological schools there is a strong tendency to treat the biblical past as if it were an authority in its own right. I suppose this is in some way functional, else it would not exist, but it seems to me nowadays ever more *dis*functional. There is a mandarin quality to all reverence toward tradition, for it requires an elite to know and "rightly" interpret what tradition holds. In cults, the elite turn out to be charismatic leaders with a cadre who hand down the "true word." In scholarly circles the elite are historians, linguists, and biblical interpreters who come to be known as experts on their subject. In the church around the corner, the power of interpretation is usually vested in the preacher, who does not often ask what the flock see in scripture but tells them what they should see. "All professions," says a character in G. B. Shaw's *The Doctor's Dilemma*, "are conspiracies against the laity." I may add that they are conspiracies against the past, too, for they seek to control what we know and think of it.

When the question arises, out of present-day circumstance, whether to ordain women to the priesthood, it becomes relevant to know what is in the Bible on the subject, not because that will settle the matter but because we need, for the sake of the church's continuity, to know whether we are to break pattern, stay within it, or modify it. The answer, in this case, is that there is nothing directly upon the question in the Bible, though there is a lot of ancillary matter about the low status of women in general. If the question is whether to countenance homosexuality, there is a lot to be found in the Bible, almost all of it negative. In both cases, the question has finally to be resolved with the aid of present conscience and wisdom, which scholarship may inform but over which it has no special competence.

In other words, historical knowledge by itself has no *moral* weight. We should remember, though, that historical knowledge "by itself" is not possible, since what we know of history is nearly the same as what we want to know. My own southern family, for instance, did not wish to know that it was descended from slave-owners, and so it happened that I neither asked nor was told that the great-grandfather for whom I am named and about whom I had been told many things was a slave-holder. This information did not become part of my known history until the 1960's, when the civil rights movement occasioned certain heated discussions with family elders which brought it to light. I was by then more than forty years old.

For me to point out that historical knowledge is correlated with present-future expectation does not mean that historical scholarship is diminished in value. It means that its value arises in a dynamic relation between one's present-future and one's past. To acknowledge that the questions and methods of historical research arise out of present-future expectancy is to revivify scholarship and give it moral value.

Nothing would be better for biblical scholarship at the present time than to listen to the churches to find out what needs to be known. This would not be easy, for the churches are so used to regarding scholars as the custodians of the past, and are so lacking in good conscience about their own authority, that they are dumbfounded by scholarship and do not trust their own ability to ask good questions. They have been too long the victims of professional conspiracy.

Neither scripture nor tradition has any authority by itself. To discuss the authority of the Bible as if the book could itself answer this question, or as if there were *a priori* theological arguments to decide the matter, is a vain enterprise. We cannot well say what authority the Bible *should* have. We can, however, observe the functioning authority it *does* have.

Whatever any party may say about the truth of scripture, all parties pick and choose their way within the canon. The famous case is Luther, who mightily invoked the authority of scripture to challenge that of Rome, yet who dismissed the Letter of James as "an epistle of straw," declared that the Word of God to Moses was not the Word to Luther, therefore not binding upon him, and in many sane ways interpreted scripture quite freshly. A fundamentalist today may claim that no one should "tamper with God's Holy Word," yet he or she will by no means feel obliged to obey all the laws of the Old Testament. I heard report of a public hearing before a California legislative panel at which a witness declared that homosexuality should be outlawed because it is condemned in the Book of Leviticus (18:22). The witness was silenced when a panelist asked if Leviticus should also be followed in its commandment to put the homosexual to death (18:29; 20:13). Christian scholars of the Bible do not accept the "authenticity" of all the passages they study, and every lay reader treats the Bible like a smorgasbord from which are selected the parts to take in and those to be discretely passed over. All readers, interpreters, and churches have a "canon within the canon," a cluster of related parts that have for them more authority than the rest.

What actual function, then, does the existence of the biblical canon serve? (This is, to my mind, more important than the related question: How did the canon come to be?) I light upon an obvious, certainly not original, answer.

The canon functions like a formal "constitution" of the church. Reference to it as authoritative for belief and practice is made in the membership and ordination vows of most churches. The canon has been invested with the authority to hold Christianity together by being treated as a necessary point of reference for all Christians. How well this works can be seen from the fact that Christianity is both schismatic and ecumenical.

I do not propose that the canon is the *only* factor holding Christianity together and animating its vision of worldwide unity. I say merely that the canon provides a kind of lowest common denominator among the denominations. It does not prevent argument; but it serves, more often than not, to establish the terms of the argument. In this sense, Christians *are* a "people of the Book," but it is important to remember that this does not necessarily mean the book is sacred.

All communities that endure very long need the "authority" of a common point of reference, either in written form like the Constitution of the United States or in an oral tradition. In this way scripture has served the whole church.

Is it good that the canon functions in this way? Does it enhance the church? My answer contains bad news and good news. The bad news first, because it's not very new.

The terrible price Christianity has paid for the maintenance of a "sacred" canon is to have ended up with a sacred cow. "The Bible says . . ." has become a stopper and an embarrassment. Not only does it inhibit the mission of the church to help liberate the oppressed, it also oppresses the church. The Bible as sacred cow requires constant feeding, care, and obeisance. Since the Enlightenment, the overburdened Bible has become decrepit. Its original languages, Hebrew and Greek, have been almost forgotten, even among well educated classes, so the people of the book have to be constantly fed on a diet of translators' milk. The Bible's joints have started to crack, owing to the kind attentions of scholarly husbandmen who have attempted by form criticism, redaction criticism, structural analysis, etc., to take the animal apart and put it back together. Every Sunday the Bible is hauled into a pulpit, held up to public view, and forced to utter something for the edification of the faithful. The book is saddled with every kind of burden, the better to show that it can do all things for all people. Finally, its usefulness declining, the Bible is put out to pasture by our culture, where it suffers the neglect of the aged. This entire spectacle is a modern scandal. It is not due primarily to the increase of "secularism." It is due most of all to the churches' having made of the Bible a fetish, a talisman, a test of one's loyalty to God. This is behavior quite unworthy of a people who are supposed to "stand fast in the freedom whereby Christ has set us free" (Gal. 5:1). The formal name for the offense is biblicism, which has adherents among both the naive and the sophisticated. The tragedy of it was well observed by the Canadian literary critic Northrop Frye when he remarked that the Bible "would still be a popular book if it were not a sacred one" (Frye 1957, p. 116).

The positive side of the matter is that the church does need a traditional, specific, intelligible document that is familiar from regular use and can be consulted in times of crisis and disagreement. The good news is that the sacred cow is *not* dead and even, from time to time, snorts its way to attention.

In this regard, I believe it very important to remember that we are talking about *canon*, about the Bible as a delimited, time-honored assemblage of specifically Jewish and Christian literature. We should not, as we are tempted to do when the Bible roars with life, change the subject to something vague like the "truth" of the "saving events" that supposedly underlie and justify the scriptures as scripture. Neither should we adopt the conservatives' version of the same idea and change the subject to God's direct inspiration of the Bible's words. The church needs a canon precisely because the truth of God and the saving activity of God in human history are matters of the most intense dispute. So divisive are they among persons and factions that they as often split the church as unite it. This should not surprise us. The closer we come to religious truth the more anxiety we find until, by grace, we may pass through the anxiety to be blessed by the fire of God. The canon is needed by the church just *because* the truth of God cannot be contained in an institution, not even, and especially, the institution which mediates that truth. Far from *being* the Word of God, scriptures are the church's shield and protection from it. Like Perseus' shield when he went to slay the Medusa, whose very look could turn him to stone, scripture (at its best) refracts and reflects the Word of God, allowing the church to approach it indirectly and thus live near holiness without perishing.

For the individual, let me add, and for some small, occasional groups, the scripture may serve a very different function. It may suddenly become transparent to the glory of God. But so may anything else.

I am speaking, then, of the theological role that scripture plays in the sociology of the church. Canon, as such, is a sociological (or, as we say, traditional) phenomenon. From this fact its theological importance arises.

To preserve ourselves from biblicism we must rid ourselves of all fancy ideas about Bible and canon. We must look at the Bible's authority using both sides of "the authority question" — the external and the internal.

Most of what I read concerning biblical and canonical authority proceeds as if that authority were a matter of external necessity: the Bible is authoritative simply because it has been given to us, like a wad of money thrust suddenly into one's hand by a stranger. Various rationalizations are offered: the Bible is the record of the "saving events"; it is the record of the *past* (all the way back to Adam and Eve), and the past is by definition authoritative; it is (here comes the *coup de grace*) THE WORD OF GOD. The message from fundamentalists and from more liberal exponents of biblical studies is often the same: the Bible stands over the church as its authority because that's the way God wants it.

No wonder the modern conscience has rebelled. The legitimate protest of the Enlightenment was against all wholly extraneous authority, not in the sense that there are not things we are compelled to do (live in the gravity field and endure the Lisbon earthquake, for example), but in the sense that an extraneous compulsion in the moral sphere becomes immoral when it claims for itself any absolute rights. Modern thought has, for good moral reason, turned this argument against kings, dictators, class privilege, patriarchy, racism, "common sense," the superego, religion, the Bible, and God.

The church has been very slow to perceive that it cannot survive the revolution in modern conscience while holding onto the notion of God as an absolute, extraneous authority, much less the Bible as the expression of that authority. I say this in spite of the fact that the more conservative and authoritarian Protestant churches are today increasing their adherents while the more liberal denominations decline. The strength of conservatives is that they at least *confront* "the authority question" and answer it clearly. Those who think their answers wrong often dodge the question. A liberalism that cannot go beyond the conservatives' view of authority is bound to suffer in times of political and social retrenchment such as we see about us today. In the long run, however, unless our civilization shall perish, the moral protests of the last four centuries against extraneous, absolutist authorities will prevail.

The church needs now to learn a lesson of psychological maturity. It should ask of scripture, "Who gave you the authority to be our text of reference?" And it should answer: "*We* did." The legitimate *external* authority, here as elsewhere, is a function of *internal* authority. "We have this treasure," said Paul, "in earthen vessels" (I Cor. 4:7). It is time to put the emphasis on "we have." This would put the church in a self-assertive position, which would make it more interesting and would be better than its usual arrogance, its claim to be able, with the aid of scripture, to speak for God. Gnosticism was better than this, for it imparted its mysteries only in secret, which shows a proper restraint concerning public claims for "the truth."

The church, broadly speaking, is the author of scriptures, and from this their authority proceeds. Certainly the church is the body that authorized the Christian canon and still today maintains it. This is what we must own up to. Doing so would free us to ask what good the scriptures are for us in the liberating work we are called to share with God in the present-future. It would also free us to see more clearly, and with less rationalization, the scriptures' liabilities. Finally, and most threatening, such ownership of authorship would make the church clearly political, for its reality would then be understood as the way it acts upon the present scene. As long as scripture is viewed as a purely external authority derived from past time, it circumvents responsibility for present action, no matter if the Bible itself calls us *to* responsibility. But the moment we view the Bible as something *we* have written, for the purpose of not forgetting the encounters we have had with God, our identity becomes more clear and we may be agents in the new work God performs today.

"My task as a theologian," writes Dorothee Sölle of her dialogue with Christian scripture and tradition, "encompasses three operations: to translate whatever can be translated into modern scientific language; to eliminate anything that contradicts a commitment to love; to name, and stupidly (*blöde*) to repeat, what I can neither translate nor put aside as superfluous" (Sölle 1975, p. 8).

The scriptures are part of our memory bank. Without them we would suffer institutional amnesia and go mad. Like everyone's memory, they contain strange things. Some of the oddities become clear upon "translation," by which Sölle means not only cross-over from Greek and Hebrew but also paraphrase and translation into action. Other oddities in scripture are positively harmful in our present context. Sölle is rightly bold, as Luther was, to say that she will not grant these authority. Finally, some parts of scripture are neither clear nor harmful, but mystifying. They are the precipitate of our past encounters with God that we cannot fathom today. We keep them and recite them "stupidly" out of awareness that our past experience, as a people, contains particles of wisdom we cannot, at this moment, consciously comprehend. As the wisdom of my body to maintain and heal itself (also to age and die) is greater than I know, so the church's scriptural memory includes mysteries greater than all prayer and scholarship can read. And as I endanger myself when I pretend to know more about my body than I do know, or to know what all the contents of my memory mean, so the church imperils itself when it pretends that it can make plain all hidden meanings of scripture. Precisely at this point, ownership and authorship become crucial. When confronted with a mystery, we have a tendency in bad faith (as Jean-Paul Sartre calls it) to disclaim responsibility. "Since we don't understand this," we are tempted to think, "we didn't write it. It has come to us from outside and is evidence of an external authority. Here the church reaches its limit, and God dictates to it as God pleases."

It is a foolishness of ego, left over from the Enlightenment, to think that our rational powers are the core of our identity. Psychology and historical research both inform us that we do many things unwittingly. It does not follow that they are not of our own authorship.

To take responsibility for the deeds, ideas, and words that proceed from us, whether we knew what we were doing or not, is a requirement if we are to enter into dialogue with the Bible and with the God represented therein. I cannot be in dialogue with anything or anybody wholly extraneous to me. To imagine so is to engage in fantasy and to head toward solipsism. The surest way to render God captive to human, ecclesiastical, or theological fantasy is to insist that God is "wholly Other." Other than what? Robbed of all context except for the negative "other," God comes quickly to resemble the who or what that God is other *than*. Karl Barth's "wholly Other" God is Barth writ large, and those who tell us that scripture is God's truth and not ours are the first to interpret its mysteries to suit them.

The way to let something or someone stand "over against" is first to identify with that thing or person. Then the drama can unfold. A channel of communication is open, and the variety and spice of the matter can be tasted, since I know that the tasting is done by *me* and is real with my reality. Dramatists have long known that the drama unfolds in the soul of the spectator. Dramatic conventions, styles, and techniques are all ways of gaining the "consent" of the audience to allow the drama to happen within them. It is as true to say that *I* kill Desdemona as to say Othello does. Unless I slay her, Othello does not. Without my consent, the play on stage is an embarrassing dumb show.

The mysteries of scripture, then, like the parts that seem plainer, are ours. We, the people who perpetuate the scriptures by reverence, rote, and fiat, did write them somewhere way back in time. By virtue of our communal memory, which is not imposed upon us but is of our own preconscious doing, they are *present* reality and part of that future world into which we are now going.

We hold this treasure, and *we* hold this earthen vessel, and it is quite within our power to drop it.

————————

Sometimes I scare myself with my view of scriptural authority. It flies in the face of the church's desire to regard the texts as some kind of legacy it must revere to the end of time. My thought denies that a Christian is obligated to believe or obey any part of the Bible just because it is there. I am offended by church vows that promise obedience to Holy Scripture as the true and sufficient source of faith and practice. I have the impression such articles are often subscribed to dishonestly, with tongue in cheek. Those vows originated, I think, at times of polemic no longer pertinent. They came from a struggle to liberate the Christian conscience from *another* external authority—that of the bishop and curia of Rome. Yet I pause now and then to wonder if we may need that polemic again, may need to sanctify the texts in order to fight off some new tyrant, as the Confessing Church in Germany did in the face of Hitler. But then I remember that "Holy Scripture" is as powerful a tool in the hands of the wicked as is "objective history" in the custody of state historians. I recall that no truth can be held pure by "objectivity." A political factor is present in any body of truth: Whose interests does it serve?

Truth is as existential as time. In coming to know anything we start with what we already know. Then we loop into the unfamiliar, returning with some of it to our starting place. We link the new knowledge with the old in a process called "assimilation" and thus enter upon a new state of knowing, wherein the old has been transformed.

How do we know what authority to give the unfamiliar? It may be illusory or poisonous—"full of lies," as people used to say. In these matters we have no choice, as far as I can see, but to rely on our appetites and our experience. We will attempt to assimilate that part of the unfamiliar that interests us, that we are drawn to by need and curiosity. Much of it we leave instinctively alone, sensing danger, until some brave Darwin, Freud, Einstein, or Jesus ventures ahead of us, moved by an appetite bolder than ours. We assimilate by testing, which is closely related to tasting. New knowledge is "proved" upon the board of experience and experiment, by trial and error. The validity of any knowledge is an existential decision made in the light of experiences old and new that so "work" for us that we refuse to deny them.

In no legitimate operation of our minds are we compelled to obey authority, testimony, or evidence against our consent. A truth not freely assented to is not a truth. As long as it is authentic, truth is inseparable from its liberating function. I will make that statement stronger: Truth *is* the liberation of the mind from all restraint by evidence or logic that does not have a self-authenticating character. This means that the authority of truth is the authority we give it when we are under no external compulsion to do so.

The identity of truth with liberation in the life of the mind is of a piece with the identity of truth and liberation in social praxis. Whoever is not freeing the neighbor from captivity is not doing the truth. Every institution and every belief is to be judged by its liberating result. Whatever does not increase the freedom of all is against the truth. Jesus said as much when he said, "the truth will make you free" (John 8:32).

As the New Testament advises us to "test the spirits to see whether they are of God," so I think we need also to test the scriptures. In fact, I believe we already do this. As I have pointed out, people pick and choose their levels of authority in the Bible, yet we rarely confess that we are doing so. It takes a Luther, a Sölle, and other bold people to say of a certain part of the Bible, "I won't pay any attention to that," though this is what the rest of us are doing all the time. The New Testament writers, in their use of the Old, did the same (Sanders 1975).

Biblical authority is of a piece with all other intellectual and moral authority. It has to do with existential truth in existential time. To use an old theological term, it is confessional. Only so can it facilitate and not corrupt the intent of the First Commandment, which is that we should love God with all our heart, mind, and strength. The love of God is not the same as the love of our memories, though the love of God may teach us to love our memories more than we often do. I regard the canon as saying to us, "Don't forget!" What it does *not* do is tell us, when we do remember, what we are now to believe and do. That requires our own freedom with God in the present-future.

The Bible is a storybook. Even the parts that read like law, psalm, prophecy, and theology are stories out of the past. The Bible is an album of the church's lore.

In my house in the country, there are some photograph albums. Whenever my children arrive there, they put on a record (also called an album) and take one of the picture books off the shelf to study it. The photos go back to my own childhood. The oldest of the books was a labor of love by my mother, storing images against the advance of time. By now my children have seen these pages scores of times, yet they study them still, and I know that some of the pictures have shaped their imaginations. However, my children do not live as I have lived, nor do they honor all the precepts of their father and their grandmother. Daily they confront questions never alive for her, nor for me. They have become what Margaret Mead once called "a frontier in time" (Mead 1970, pp. 65–97). They know more about the culture in which they live than I do, for the culture has changed faster than I, who was born in a different time. Yet pictures and tales from the old times matter to my children. They live in a storied world. If they remember some of the past, and if they are not forced to obey it, they will add new stories of their own.

By the addition of new stories, old stories live and change. Without addition, old stories die. The past needs the present-future so as to be resurrected from the grave of oblivion.

If the Christ of the church is nothing other than Christ past, if Christ cannot be added to, cannot change, cannot transcend the scriptural legacy, that Christ is dead. To avoid worship of a dead man, I take my stand with my Christian ancestors who proclaimed a resurrected Christ. This means also a Christ transformed. The Christ of such a faith encounters us in our present-future with challenge to set all prisoners free.

·6·

Spirit, God, and Christ
Toward a Trinitarian Ethic

Relatedness is the subject of the doctrine of Trinity. In line with the importance I attached to relativity theory in Chapter 4, I turn directly to Trinity in the constructive part of my christological work, which will occupy this and the next two chapters.

After I had given a series of lectures critical of traditional teachings about Christ as center, model, norm, and "once-for-all," a questioner stood up. "What," he inquired, "are you going to do about the problem of relativism?" I replied that I intended to embrace it: for me it was not a problem but an occasion for insight. He was surprised and confused. As he told me later, he had always assumed that faith and morals were being eroded by modern relativism.

It is true that there is a kind of relativism which amounts to "anything goes," and so prevalent is that connotation of the word that I once thought I should repudiate relativism altogether. I have decided, however, that it is more honest to affirm it. After all, relativism means (denotes) a belief in relativity, a belief that things are and are known in relation to each other. If I believe in some kind of relativity, I am in that regard a relativist; and if I believe, as I do, that God and life are fundamentally relational, I am a thoroughgoing relativist.

My christological task therefore is to understand Christ in relativistic terms. I must think of Christ *relative to* God and the world.

It is not Christ *per se* who will then occupy me, nor God in Godself, nor the world in itself, nor me in myself. What will concern me as a relativist is relationality; and that is why, for the constructive side of my task, I turn to the Christian doctrine of Trinity. I shall, to be sure, attempt to cast it in a light it did not have in ancient times, but I am both aware and grateful that Christian thinkers in the formative period of church doctrine sought a way to express the creative relationality of God. They were the Christian relativists of their age, who shocked the absolute monotheists around them.

"Trinity" soon became orthodox. After that, it became arcane. During the Enlightenment it was ridiculed. Modern Christians who want to be rational and practical leave it aside. It tends to be prized only by traditionalists, who defend it as a great mystery of the faith. That it is still a radical doctrine, perhaps more valid in an age of relativity than ever before is not a widespread thought. I venture to treat it so, hoping to find in trinitarian thinking the spur for a dynamic and ethical teaching about Christ.

Without its doctrine of Trinity, I do not imagine that Christianity would have survived. The doctrine enabled the church not only to say that Jesus was God incarnate (a fragile claim in itself and not a very original one to be made about a religious hero) but to regard the divinity of Christ Jesus in very creative terms. Trinity is not only a way of understanding God and Christ. It is fundamentally a conception of life. I propose to look at it from two points of view: as a philosophical concept relevant to life in general, and as an ethical concept assisting Christians to decide what is good. Its bearing upon christology will emerge in reference to these themes.

In familiar language, trinitarian doctrine says that God exists in three "persons." The identification of the three as Father, Son, and Holy Spirit constitutes a problem I shall set aside for the moment, promising to return to it shortly. My initial interest is in the word "person" and in the apparent paradox of asserting that one God is three. Why would theologians have asserted that one is three, three is one, and that the three are "persons"? And why does a twentieth-century pragmatist like me find this ancient conundrum in some way relevant to the ethical crises of our time?

The brief answer is that trinitarian thought is a corrective to all forms of dualism. The meaning and relevance of this will be seen when I come to the ethical dimension of the doctrine, in this chapter and in the two that follow. Meanwhile, I must show what fundamental sense there is in a trinitarian view of reality. Unless the idea makes sense to our minds, it will not bear ethical weight, nor will it be convincing in our understanding of a transformed Christ. The ancient church proposed the doctrine as an inscrutable mystery, known only by divine revelation. This is not the approach I shall take. I regard Trinity as profoundly rational.

The import of the word "person" in the doctrine of Trinity is twofold. First, it insists radically upon the *personification* of God, and hence of all life. Second, it drives one to regard life as *relationship*. It was these two ideas, taken together, which led to the number *three* in dialectical relation to *one*. In other words, a trinity is implied in any relationship that is understood as personal. When this concept is applied to God, as it was in the formative period of Christian theology, it implies that all life and all reality have the character of "personal" relations. This idea posed a sharp challenge to Greek philosophy and is equally radical in the eyes of most philosophy and some science today.

My use of the word "personal" is subject to misunderstanding, owing to a connotation the word has acquired in modern usage. That it has done so is itself evidence of the decay of trinitarian thinking over the centuries.

We have come to associate "personal" with "private," customarily contrasting a "personal" relation with a public one. What I eat for breakfast, my sex life, what I confide to my friend, and so on are understood as "personal" matters, while the authoring of a book, the teaching of a course, and campaigning for the ERA are public. Industrialized societies have pretty well divorced "public" from "personal," and the depth psychologies of Freud and Jung, not to mention a great mass of bourgeois art and literature, have helped them to do it. The idea that the public person is no less real, perhaps more so, than the private person has become foreign to us, especially if we belong or wish to belong to the middle class. The topic has been well treated by Hannah Arendt in *The Human Condition* (1958) and more popularly by Philip Slater in *The Pursuit of Loneliness* (1970).

The divorce of the "personal" from the "public" has contributed to the modern idea that nature is impersonal. After all nature is the most public of all domains. It is what belongs to everybody and therefore to nobody in particular. To have a "personal" relation with nature is thought to be romantic self-indulgence. We have removed the idea of "person" far from everything that stands in broad daylight for public view. Such was not the case when the Patristic theologians spoke of God as a trinity of three "persons." They certainly did not mean to suggest three private, autonomous individuals.

How far removed early trinitarian thought was from modern ideas of autonomy and personality may be seen in the fact that the discussions then oscillated between reference to three divine *prosopa* (persons) and three *hypostases* (substances). Gradually the two words came to mean almost the same, so that the Latin word *persona* was often used to translate either one.

The preference of the Latin-speaking theologians for *persona* rather than *substantia* has had profound effect upon European and American thought, leading to religious, philosophical, legal, and aesthetic reflection upon the idea of personhood. It prepared the way for modern psychology and existentialism, not to mention the dramatic genius of Shakespeare. Until the idea of personhood was overtaken by industrialism and veered off into bourgeois privatism, it was one of Christianity's greatest contributions to culture, in spite of the fact that Christianity has also fostered, as I noted in an earlier chapter, a pernicious attitude toward some groups as nonpersons.

When we think of "substance," we think either of physical material or of material for thought. So did the Greeks when they said *hypostasis* and the Romans when they said *substantia*. If I say that a book is substantial, I probably mean it contains material for thought, but I might mean it has many pages and is large enough to use as a doorstop. If I say of anything that it has no substance, I mean there is nothing to it. The substance of anything is its reality, as opposed to its mere appearance or its form alone. We may see pictures in clouds, but we do not imagine them to have much substance. When the Greek theologians said that God exists in three *hypostases* (substances), they meant that God has three realities, each as real as the others. They did *not* mean, as they frequently insisted, that God has merely three ways of appearing, three guises, so to speak. The reduction of Trinity to a matter of appearances was called *modalism* and was rejected. It is then something of a shock to discover that *hypostasis* was translated by the Latin *persona*, and that *persona* denoted a part of a theatrical costume! A *persona* was the mask customarily worn by an actor in a theater. How could the word which means substance also mean a covering for the face?

Persona is a noun derived from the verb *personare*, which means to sound (*sonare*) through (*per*). The mask worn by Greek and Roman actors in the large amphitheaters was constructed so as to serve as a megaphone, projecting the actor's voice all over the outdoor theater. The mask was also designed to project a visual image of the character being portrayed. Together, these two functions of the mask were to convey to the spectator the *substance* of the portrayal. They helped to manifest, for eye and ear, the substance which the spectator was supposed to "get." Without them the spectator might see and hear little and go home not having grasped what the performance was about.

In the word *persona*, then, the reality and the means of its projection coalesce. When the actor masks himself, he is not hiding: he is revealing what he is about. It is important to note that the substance revealed by the mask is not static. If it were, the mask could only hide it. If what is real is already there, *under* the mask, the mask is a disguise; but if the reality is what the masker is *up to*, is what he or she wishes to bring about, is indeed the very act of bringing it about (which is always the case in theater), then the mask is anything but a disguise; it is an essential part of the dynamic reality. With this thought we are not yet at a doctrine of Trinity, but we have already posed a challenge to any dualism predicated on the difference between appearance and reality, as if there were some kind of reality that is different from its appearance. Such challenge to dualism by profound understanding of what a performer's mask does is a feature trinitarian theology shares with primitive religions, which usually attribute great meaning to masks and carve them with astonishing artistry.

I do not know exactly when the word *persona* lost its denotation of actor's mask in favor of its reference to what we call a "person." In classical Latin it carried both senses. The theologians' use of it in discussions of God helped to shift its primary meaning from that of "revealing mask" to that of "no mask at all." Our habit today, by a combination of industrialism, individualism, and Christian exaltation of "the person," is to think that the real person is naked and alone, all else about him or her being the accretion of "merely" social behavior. We have drifted far from primitive religion, from trinitarian thought, and from communitarian life.

I must attempt to remind my reader of the most vital sense of what it is like to be a person. Only by doing this can I make it clear why and how the doctrine of Trinity insists upon the personification of God and all of life.

If we recall the occasions when we have felt ourselves to be most personally alive, we find that what we remember is ourselves in the presence of someone (or something) intensely *with* us. If you are a public performer of any kind, you may recall moments when you and your audience achieved a fine rapport. If you shy from public display, you may recall certain moments of intimacy with friend, family, or lover. If you are a very solitary person, you may recall the woods you walked in, the darkness about you, or the crowded street on which you felt the more alone because there were so many there to surround your isolation. We know our loneliness by reference to what we are *with*, even if sometimes we are most conscious of being *without*. Nothing is experienced except in relation, however various our relations may be. Trinitarian thought goes one step further: Nothing *is* except in relation, and fundamentally all relations are like those between persons.

When I am in the presence of my friend, my mask and my self come together. I am intensely alive. So is he. As he is my friend, I have no need to disguise anything, no need to lie or put on a "good" face. When we first became friends, I said, "I feel as if I could tell you whatever comes into my mind," and he answered, "So do I." At the same time, this feeling of candor has another side. My friend not only permits me to be honest: he summons me to it. He seldom does it by injunction, though he will occasionally say, "Come off it." He does it mostly by being there. I respond to his presence by desiring to project myself, make myself open, be near and clear. I put on for him a face that is more real than the one I lapse into when he is gone. It has more of me in it.

The same thing happens when I work "alone." Writing this book, or making prints in the darkroom, I come to myself by concentration on what I am working *with*. Photographers say they put an exposed piece of paper in the developing tray and wait for it to "sing." They're not crazy, and they're not just darkroom poets. They are giving voice to their experience of what is *with* them. The reality is the transaction "between."

If we do not personify what we're with, we lose it. If I "thingify" my friend, he goes dead, or runs away. It's not as if I encountered real "persons" one moment and real "things" the next. Their personhood and their thinghood do not belong to them alone. They belong to their relation to what they're *with*. It is not possible simply to *be* a person. One can only *become* a person, never finished, and the way to do it is to personify whatever we meet. "Person" is a way of relating. "Thing" is another way. "In the beginning is the relation."

I have spoken of "the relation" as if "it" were one-on-one. One and one equal two. We are not yet at trinitarian thought, though we have begun at the right place, the idea that a person is a self only in relation. The next step is to see what such a relation involves.

In every relation of one to one, a third element is present. There is no way for one to relate to another without "something else" coming up, and this not as a mere distraction but as the necessary condition and consequence of the relation. Every dyad turns out to be a tryad. We may dream of "a bicycle built for two," but then it turns out that we cannot get rid of the bicycle.

A couple decide to hitch up, steal away, and live in a shack in the woods. The next thing they know, they are having to repair the shack.

Two lovers look raptly into each others' eyes. The next thing they know, they are talking about some movie they saw. If not that, they talk about the "love" they made half an hour ago, or the food in the refrigerator, or the music on the radio, or the warmth of the bed they're in. They cannot remain in relation to each other if they do not refer to something "else."

A Sandinista rebel in Nicaragua confronts the National Guard. This relation is more of hate than of love. It makes no sense unless they refer to the "others" whom their confrontation is about.

A prisoner stands before a judge. The two are locked in their roles. It is a charade unless they can both appeal to something "else," which is either expediency or justice.

A scientist observes certain data in the laboratory. She records the data. The information makes no sense unless it can be referred to something "else," which is called a theory.

One plus one equals nothing unless there is something "else," which we call arithmetic or mathematics.

Every relation requires a context. The minute we understand reality as the relation of one to another, we discover a relational field giving substance to the relation. The field is not *prior* to the relation. It is with it, about it, around it, in it. It is the field *of* that relation.

The philosophical point in all this is difficult to state because it hinges on prepositional phrases. We are educated to think that those little words called prepositions have only minor significance in a sentence. The trumpets of sentences, we learn at school, are subject, verb, and predicate. Prepositions are like little noises made by flutes or tinkling triangles. Their place in a syntactical diagram of the sentences is off to the side. What one sees in the corner of one's eye cannot be all that important. One shouldn't make much of it in a philosophy or a psychology.

Taking my cue from Gestalt psychologists, I shall proceed by thinking about the corner of the eye and what is known as peripheral vision, which turns out to be vital for seeing.

When our eyes fasten, even for an instant, upon an object, we do not know what we are seeing if we see the object "alone." To know what the object is, we have to see it in relation to its surrounding field. Experiments have demonstrated this. It may happen that the surrounding field is not visible, either because of an impairment in one's visual system or because the experimenter has contrived a situation in which the subject seems to be free of any environment. In these cases, the subject will either not recognize the object at all or will supply a context by imagination in order to interpret—that is, to "see"—the object. This explains why any loss of peripheral vision is so hazardous. The surrounding field has to be guessed at. If the guess is wrong, one may easily fall off a cliff or be struck by a car. We call the condition "partial blindness," and we may express it more precisely as loss of ability to make sense of the field one is in.

Gestalt psychology, which is a kind of epistemology, proposes that all our knowing requires the identification of an object (which may also be called a "subject") in relation to a contextual field. It refers to the object of our knowing as *figure*, the contextual field as *ground*; and it holds that the two are correlated in any act of knowing. The ground is ground inasmuch as it is ground *of* the figure. The figure is figure inasmuch as it becomes differentiated *from* the ground while also belonging *to* it. Knowledge is relational, for the good reason that it has to do with interaction between knower, known, and context.

I suppose that all theories of knowledge are relational theories, for they have to reckon with a knowing subject and a known object. Gestalt theory emphasizes that the relation is triadic: the knower, the known, and their common contextual field or ground. Furthermore, none of these is static. Our knowledge consists of interpretation of *changing* relations among all three. Since the time of Parmenides and Plato, several theories of knowledge have also been triadic. They have usually differed from Gestalt theory, however, in two respects: (1) they have tended to regard the contextual field as *a priori* and static, a *given*; (2) they have attempted to make the context itself an object of knowledge, as if by reason and contemplation we could bring to focus what we are aware of only at the edge of our vision. Gestalt theory reminds us that if we bring to focus what is peripheral, it now becomes a figure and is intelligible only against some *other* ground, *ad infinitum*. Infinity, as I argued in Chapter 4, is an entailment *of* finitude. Finitude is delineation *from* infinity *in* the address of one finite thing *to* another. The reality is relational, and the relations are expressed with prepositions. There is no substance of any kind, not even an ontological substance and certainly not a divine substance, prior to relating.

The similarity of the foregoing ideas to trinitarian thought may be obvious. Gestalt psychologists do not, of course, employ their scheme theologically, but I shall do so.

Trinitarian doctrine was never meant to identify *who* the persons of the Trinity are. That had already been done in the New Testament's references to God, Christ, and Spirit. The doctrine was meant to throw light on their "substance" by seeing their relation. It did so by holding that they are co-divine, co-equal and co-eternal. This led to the somewhat mystical formula of "three in one, one in three." The formula remains opaque as long as there is any sugges- tion that any of the three persons is unchanging; for if that were so, their dynamic relatedness would not be intelligible. There is no doubt that the early trinitarian theologians failed to see this point clearly. They were generally committed to the idea that God is above time. They spoke of "Him" as timeless, impassable, and with- out direction (*a-tropos*). They did not seem to realize that such a view of God makes a genuine Trinity impossible. It is a near- miracle that they thought of Trinity at all, which they themselves recognized by calling it a divinely revealed mystery.

It was Augustine, in the fifth century, who came close to the interpretation of Trinity I advocate here, and this in spite of his strongly held view of God's timelessness. Augustine defined Holy Spirit as the love that exists between the Father and the Son:

> And if the charity whereby the Father loves the Son and the Son loves the Father displays, beyond the power of words, the communion of both, it is most fitting that the Spirit who is common to both should have the special name of charity. (*De Trinitate*, p. 165)

This passage and similar ones in *De Trinitate* hint at an under- standing of Spirit as the contextual bond shared by the first and second Persons of the Trinity. Their relation, Augustine intuited, is grounded in love, which provides the holy context for their divinity. Few stronger statements about love have ever been made. The ambience giving substance to all reality is here personified as holy love. The thought shows a deeply trinitarian awareness.

A doctrine of the Trinity of God requires two divine figures related in a contextual field that is itself divine. In other words, the logic requires two figures of a definite character and a third com- ponent that is ineffable. The genius of trinitarian theology was to have seen that none of the three has priority. This was expressed in the words "co-equal" and "co-eternal." It was an error to have com- promised this point with the linear terms "First, Second, and Third" Persons, putting God the Father first, Christ second, and

Spirit third. The Western church, greatly at odds with the Eastern on the point and sowing the seed of an eventual schism, inserted the word *Filioque* into the Nicene Creed, to indicate that the Spirit proceeds from the Son as well as the Father. Unfortunately, the result, whether intended or not, was to subordinate Spirit to Christ, reinforcing the linear conception of the First, Second, and Third Persons. This ordering subverted trinitarianism with a hierarchical principle that does not belong to it at all, in fact ruins it and turns it into a mystification.

The hierarchical principle that has long contaminated trinitarianism has many bad effects, of which I shall mention two. The first is a powerful reinforcement of sexism. In the moment in which Trinity is imagined as a hierarchy with a first, a second, and a third person, it falls prey to the sexual hierarchy of culture, particularly the idea of primogeniture. Suddenly the Father is not simply the divine figure whom the Son loves but is the *One* alone from whom all else "proceeds." The Son becomes the heir, the first-born prince. And Spirit, the ineffable component, therefore associated by sexism with femininity, comes last. So understood, Trinity provided a potent rationale for masculine primacy. It subordinated feminine quality to masculine substance, so to speak, excluding the thought of *woman* from the idea of God completely. I do not mean, of course, that woman was not already excluded from the idea of God in Judaism, early Christianity, and Hellenistic philosophy. I mean she was now firmly locked out by a new bolt on the door, the hierarchical interpretation of Father, Son, and Spirit. Trinity, which should have celebrated the openness of God to all creation, was reduced to the model of an exclusive, all-male society. In this period, women also ceased to be church ministers (Fiorenza 1978) and the move to rid male priests of their wives began (Barstow 1979, pp. 31–36).

A second, closely related, ill effect of the hierarchical principle was the idea that the First Person of the Trinity, unlike the other two, was outside of time. This flew in the face of the statement that all three Persons were "co-eternal." The desire to have some component of God on top of time, so to speak, pushed the Trinity skyward. It seemed not enough to say, as trinitarian logic would have it, that God and creation exist in mutual recognition. God had in some way or other to be "above" creation, "above" space and time. The meaning of Christ, however, was God *in* time and space. And so was Spirit, which referred to the continuing historical presence of God, however ineffable. Trinity seemed then to involve a tension between *above* and *within*. The solution reached was not very democratic, for instead of the two immanent Persons pulling the transcendent Person in their direction, the opposite occurred. Christ and Spirit were lifted skyward. The paradox of Christ's being both in and outside of time was resolved by putting Christ at the still center of time, as I have previously said. Spirit became unearthly and of ever less importance. A hierarchical principle cannot make very much of a reality like Spirit which is impossible to locate.

If we are today to think in trinitarian terms, and if we are to find this liberating, as I think we can, we must be radical about it. We must appreciate how radical a conception it was, and still is, when it is not subverted by a hierarchical principle and by overdefinition.

Aware of the infinite context of life, human beings have a desire to close it off. One's mind cannot dwell upon infinity. We need finite figures. The usual religious or theological way to "close off" infinity is to call it "God," a word which acts as a stopper.

In *Patterns of Grace* (pp. 152f.) I noted that we tend to use the word "God" in contradictory ways, now as figure and now as ground. It is not logically possible, I said, for it to have both meanings at once. The primary connotation of "God" in all religious language is that of some definite figure: creator, lawgiver, redeemer, etc. For this reason, to speak of God as the infinite context of life can be very misleading. It often has the consequence of reducing the infinite ground of life to a finite figure, framing our infinite horizon within a clear religious limit.

The doctrine of Trinity was designed to prevent this happening, but it loses the power to do so when it is mixed with a hierarchical principle. In the history of the doctrine, "God" has come to mean the single source of everything, Christ has come to mean the man at God's right hand, and Spirit has come to suggest a more vague figure darting in and out of human experience to produce unusual behavior.

I suggest that the indeterminate quality of the word "Spirit" makes it appropriate as a name for the infinite contextual ground of life. Spirit is that meaningful power of God's life which is infinite and which resists figuration because its function is to provide meaning and power *to* the figures we encounter. The word "God" is then the more free to do what it usually does, to stand for the divine figure who confronts us with specific acts of creation, mercy, redemption, and sometimes terror. When it is clear to us that the Spirit of God is beyond all limitation, we may with less embarrassment think of God as a delimited person, just as I may be clearer about my own personal actions when I am aware of their grounding in my freedom of spirit. I and my actions are finite, but my spirit is not. Inasmuch as I am a person, my actions are definite while my spirit is beyond definition. This is why my "person" should be regarded ethically as inviolable. It is also why love for one's neighbor and love for God are alike. I cannot love Spirit as such. I can only love someone (or something) who is *of* Spirit. Healthy respect for the Spirit of God liberates the figure (stories) of God from vagueness and allows us to worship the person of God without fear of idolatry. It also motivates us to esteem our neighbor, who is figured to our eyes within the same infinite Spirit as is God. The motive for loving the neighbor and loving God becomes the same: it is the Spirit they are both *of*.

Radical trinitarianism implies that there can be no *one* definition of God. The moment we say God is this, that, or the other, we dare not stop, as if the sentences were simply true. Moreover, the reason no simple sentence about God is sufficient is not that our finite minds have to resort to inadequate symbols. The reason is that God is not one thing, or one quality, or one Person, or one principle, or even one mystery. For example, when Paul Tillich said that we can call God "Being itself" and that this is a literal, not a symbolic statement, he later took it back, saying the statement is both symbolic and nonsymbolic (Tillich 1951, p. 238; cf. 1957, p. 9). I suggest that he was wrong both times. In both instances he dreamed, as so many do, of a simple truth about God subsisting somewhere at or beyond the limits of our finite minds. We know that we are complex, we are limited, and so is life; but we dream that God is not. I call this partial, not radical, trinitarianism. Taken radically, trinitarianism means that although God is not three different Gods, neither is God always and everywhere the same. In other words, God is changeful and complex, like life. Tillich knew that Trinity is a way of speaking of God as living, but he represented this as a modification of the essence of God (Tillich 1951, pp. 228f.). A similar error is made by process theology, following Whitehead, when it speaks of God's changelessness as primordial and the changing as consequent (Whitehead 1929, pp. 46–50). More traditional theologies attempt to remove God from change altogether, the better to contrast "Him" with us.

Radical trinitarianism begins with God *in relation* to creatures, not before. (This is also where the Book of Genesis begins, as do the synoptic gospels.) Radical trinitarianism sees in Christ a figure momentarily representative of all creation. It affirms mutual recognition and mutual transaction between God and world. It perceives that this relation, like all others of a personal or reciprocal kind, carries with it a sense of ineffable presence and inexhaustible meaning. It then makes a bold theological leap. It concludes that God is no more in one part of this triad than another. To use the analogy of seeing: God is the one who sees, the one seen, and the light between them. In this sense, God is "all," but not all at once, for if the difference ceased, God would cease. To use the analogy of language: God is the speaker, the hearer, and the "sense" in between; but not all at once, for if the difference ceased, there would be no word. To use the analogy of action: God is the doer, the thing done to, and the rapture in between; but not all at once, for if the difference ceased, God would be impotent. Who then are we? We are the ones who recognize our own image in God, are recognized by it, and are the holy fear in between; but not all at once, for if the difference ceased, we would disappear in our solitude.

The history of theology is full of debate about *imago Dei*, humanity as the "image of God" (Gen. 1:26). Are we like God? Do we represent God? If so, how? Were we like God before the Fall and are we now some kind of a broken or deformed image? Do we project upon God our own image, God being nothing but the ideal of ourselves?

I propose the following: humanity is "image" of God as friend is image of friend, or even as enemy is image of enemy. As my image, my friend does not have to be "like" me, though it's a help, as long

as he or she is not *too much* like me. The same may be said of my
enemy. To have a friend or an enemy, two things are required: we
have to be interested in each other, and we have to have a common
field of action and meaning. My friend is my "image" inasmuch as
she or he is the subject of my concern, the "figure" I want to attend
to. So is my enemy. *Imago Dei*, I submit, has little (some, of course,
but little) to do with likeness. It has more to do with interest.

Humanity is the image of God inasmuch as we are God's interest,
no more and no less. I might say we are God's concern if that word
did not carry the strong connotation of "worry." To be sure, there is
a lot in us to worry about, but interest is not limited to worry.
What's vital to interest is the spark of recognition.

God is the image of humanity insofar as God interests us. Where
this interest is lost, as among so many people today, the image of
God fades. It can be restored not by theology, not by theory, not by
exhortation, not by art or human education, but only by God's
doing such things as may attract our attention. I take this to be a
biblical understanding. In Genesis, God creates Adam and Eve as a
matter of divine interest. Certainly no other motive is given. There-
after, the interest of the people of Israel in God results from God's
activity. Although the Old Testament repeatedly describes God as
"faithful," it does not represent God as immutable. Such a figure
would dissolve into the ground for lack of interest.

In Jesus, the gospels suggest, God's interest in humanity and a
human interest in God (both personified in Jesus) took a leap across
the sparking gap and made lightning. The result was a kind of
identity between them. That would be their business and would not
matter very much to us if we did not know that we and our world
belong to the contextual ground of the mutual interest between
Jesus and God. Reading the gospels, one is tempted to think Jesus
was obsessed with God, maybe God with Jesus. What held their
mutual attraction back from "obsession" was their keen awareness,
as the Gospels tell it, of the wide human/divine context that gave
their interest meaning. That is why Jesus could say that the love of
God and the love of neighbor are alike and are the whole of the law
and the prophets (Mark 12:29–31; Matt. 22:37–39). The love affair
between God and Jesus is exhilarating because its intensity is
matched by its nonexclusive character. This comes close to obses-

sion, but the real name for it, as was noticed long ago, is passion.

The ethical importance of trinitarian thinking as I have approached it may already be clear, but some aspects of it need emphasis. A temptation of the church is to turn the passion between Jesus and God into an obsession of belief. The church becomes fascinated by perpetual repetition of that one event, propounding doctrines of its immortal character. The very life of Jesus acquires a sacrosanct character. People try to imitate Jesus. Scriptural words about him become holy. Bread and wine for the communion table become sacred, and "bad" people are accused of stealing them. The name of Jesus is invoked like magic, as if to "call" upon it will save one from harm. Scholars devote their lives to the reconstruction of Jesus' "historical" life, like tourists who think they are closer to God if they make pilgrimage to the Holy Land. The difference between faith and mere religion is the difference between interest, which leads to innovation, and obsession, which leads to compulsive repetition. Jesus was an innovator.

If we are obsessive, we will insist that because Jesus was a male the image of God in Christ is forever manly. We will also insist that there can be only *one* Christ. What Jesus did is the way it *must* be done. What he *was* is how it *is*. Obsession cannot get off the dime. That is not trinitarian thinking, and it is not ethical.

The ethical value of trinitarian thought is its insight that Spirit is concomitant with passionate interest in *present* reality in the context of infinite Spirit. "Transcendence is radical immanence" (see above, p. 76). Commitment to one's friend (or one's enemy) has religious substance insofar as its context has no limit. An ethical commitment remains open to re-formation by the ingathering of new life. The new, swarming in from the edges of vision, is as godly as the old that we already have in focus. It is unethical to impose the past like a norm upon the present-future, for that is to claim that we know the full context of our encounters with our neighbors, which is an offense against Spirit. Spirit is the "more" of any relation. The ethical person will be keenly aware of Spirit and for that very reason will not claim to know it directly. When Christian theology put Christ Jesus at the center of time, regarding his unity with God as forever decisive, it put a frame around the divine/human context, setting limits to Spirit. Its ethics have been crippled ever since.

Another way of looking at the ethical value of radical trinitarianism is to see the corrective it provides for dualistic thinking. By dualism I mean any analysis of reality or of an ethical problem as if it were composed of two, and only two, fundamental principles. For example, to regard human nature as a blend of spirit and matter is dualistic. In the realm of morals, a persistent dualism has been the division of the world into good and evil forces. Sexism is maintained by dualistic mythologies of masculine and feminine. Racism similarly is nourished by an ideology of dark and light. Much social ethics, on the left and on the right, insists on dividing the world's population into the rich and the poor, the haves and the have-nots. This naive conception is based on a dualistic truism: up is different from down. The United States-Soviet arms race, which will destroy us all if it continues, is rationalized by a dualistic conception of capitalism and communism, or else of freedom and tyranny.

A dualism that has hampered much ethical thought is to regard human actions and human institutions as split between the ideal and the real. In this case, ethical theory proceeds by envisioning the ideal, then attempting to articulate principles of action to bring the real as close to the ideal as possible. A more cynical version of the same approach, calling itself "realistic," settles for principles to guard the real from becoming less ideal (worse) than it already is.

The fault in all dualistic ethics is lack of ability to envision and properly value the new. Dualisms are inherently analytic. They seek to identify the already-existent principles which define reality. Then the ethicist works as well as possible within those terms. I would be foolish to deny all validity to this, or to analytic thought generally. However, analysis is necessarily confined to what is already at hand. One cannot analyze the future except by supposing it will be like what we already know or will follow directions already known. Analytic thought in ethics is inherently conservative, even if the ethicist's political sympathies happen to be progressive. (Incidentally, our tendency to divide political life into conservative/progressive is also dualistic.) We cannot and should not eschew analysis and all conceptual dualisms. The task is to transcend them, starting with the recognition that they are not ethically adequate, even if at one stage of thought they are necessary. We need to see clearly that the identification of two leading principles in a situation, even if the two are Good and Evil, is not in itself an ethical judgment. It is not even the foundation for one because, in itself, it cannot say what the opposition between Good and Evil *means* nor what action is appropriate. Dualisms do not touch the heart of ethics, which is creative action.

In any dualism, one of the two principles will be considered better than the other. Good is "obviously" better than evil, the ideal better than the real, etc. Our culture has assumed for millennia that masculine is better than feminine. Occasionally, still within the dualistic frame, these values get reversed. Jean Genet, Charles Baudelaire, and others praise evil. Mary Daly regards feminine as better than masculine, which she has come to regard as evil (Daly 1978). In his early writings, James Cone opposed white supremacy by identifying black with God and white with the devil (Cone 1969, p. 150). To these reversals, especially concerning race and sex, the liberal democratic response is to affirm equality. All people are to be the same: white and black, male and female. By this fancy, the dualism is simply to be eliminated. Luckily, this does not occur. If it did, life would stop.

The dialectical logic of Hegel, to which I referred in Chapter 4, and which is derived from trinitarianism, is a step beyond dualism. It envisions not the elimination of antinomies in any historical situation but their transcendence in a new synthesis, the emergence of a situation that is genuinely new in relation to what has gone before. The analytic posture of dualism here passes over into a synthetic (creative) expectation which is characteristic of trinitarian thought. My present interest, however, is not in the Hegelian dialectic itself nor in the adaptation of it by Karl Marx which has changed the course of our history. I am interested in the value of radical Christian trinitarianism for ethics.

My point has to do with the "more" of any relation, to which I referred earlier. A Christian trinitarian ethic, having analyzed the given components of any situation, will then address itself to what is not yet known because it is not yet actual. Its awareness of the "more" at the edge of vision, which it will interpret theologically as

Spirit, will inform its ethical judgment. There is no way Spirit can *determine* the ethical judgment, for Spirit is indeterminate. Nevertheless, every present understanding and every specific counsel or guiding principle is informed by expectation. Trinitarian ethic communicates the expectation, not merely to acknowledge one's bias, but as necessary *meaning* of the ethic. If the expectation does not include a new reality not yet experienced, it is neither Christian nor trinitarian. If it does not make use of analysis of present circumstance, including the history of this present, it is fanciful. Trinitarian ethic makes radical commitment to the present-future. Its sense of the future is informed by its vibrant awareness of an infinite "more" contextualizing the immediate present and its history.

Jesus spoke of the world (he said kingdom) of God in apparent contradiction: it is yet to come, you know not when, and it is "among" you. The horizon of our present life has special affinity with our future, and both are "of God." No ethic that is *merely* conservative or merely private is trinitarian.

My thought on these matters is similar to the "theology of hope" pioneered by Jürgen Moltmann (1967). I am glad to acknowledge my debt to it, even though my own route to the emphasis I place on the future has been a different one. I do not like the word "hope" in this context, and I do not think the idea of "promise" is adequate to what the gospel proclaims. Both words suggest a far too linear conception, as if we live now in hope for what has in the past been promised, awaiting a future fulfillment. This makes our present time an interim between the promise and its reward, an interim of *pathos* that has received classic depiction in Samuel Beckett's *Waiting for Godot* (1953). As the interim is long, time acquires a negative value. This is always the case with the word "hope," which St. Paul used because he was having to wait so long for "the redemption of our body" (Rom. 8:16–25). Hope has a negative connotation because its opposite, by which a hopeful person is ever haunted, is despair.

I look for a word in which the positive and negative come more productively together. The one I find is "expectation." I wish it were as pithy as "hope," but it's the best I have found. St. Paul also uses it in the passage cited above: "the earnest expectation of the creature waits for the manifestation. . . ."

A lover waits for his beloved to arrive. Unless he is in despair, he does not hope to see her: he expects to.

The lovers meet and afterwards make love. They move toward climax. If their love is strong, they do not hope for climax: they expect it. Were they to hope for it, they would prevent its occurrence.

A Roman military man comes to see Jesus. His servant is ill, and he wants Jesus to perform a cure. He explains that as a military officer he can tell people what to do and they do it; he looks now to Jesus to get results. Jesus says, "I have not found such faith in Israel" (Matt. 8:3-10; Luke 7:1-9). That soldier did not hope: he expected.

A player on the basketball court reaches for the ball on the rebound. If he is a good player, not a bad one whom the coach will later dress down, he does not hope to catch the ball: he expects to.

A pianist is in the middle of a brilliant cadenza. It needs a conclusion, when the orchestra can come in. If she is good, she does not hope for a brilliant finish: she expects it. The expectation challenges her to rise to the music. Hope would cause her to falter. It would throw the orchestra.

Resistance fighters are lost if they hope. Only their expectation tells them what to do. Pregnant women do not hope to give birth, unless they dread it. They are, as used to be said, "expectant" mothers.

Hope is always *against*. The best we can say of hope is that it is "hope against hope." Expectation leans *into* the movement it is *with*. (Once more, the prepositions are telling the story.) Expectation is what Jesus called faith. When he said, "Oh ye of little faith," he suggested, "Oh you who hope for much and expect little."

If I expect my daughters and my son to live life well, I am not hoping. I am putting faith in them. What if they crash? Shall I then hope? Yes, if I lose faith. Little good will my hope do them. They need my faith, as I need theirs. The resurrection of Jesus came not by hope but by faith.

Christian ethic does not settle for making the best of a bad situation, as all dualisms do. Neither is it content to hope for a new situation. It encourages people to behave as they do behave when they expect the world of God.

In light of such ethic I shall in the next chapter turn my attention again to Christ by way of a particular ethical question: What are we to make of sex in the world of God, and what can sex tell us to expect of a present-future Christ?

·7·

Woman, Man, and Christ
Emergent Sexuality

It is not for our fathers—even our biblical fathers—to determine what the truth is now.

(Dennis Nineham 1976, p. 222)

At earlier times in my life I have tried to reconcile my sexual experiences with my fidelity to Christ Jesus, but this has failed. The longer I have lived, the more frustrating the attempt has been. The very idea of a Christian sexuality has become more and more baffling. When I hear other churchgoers express their thoughts and when I read what has been written about Christianity and sex, I conclude that we are all in a state of bafflement.

The New Testament is mostly mute concerning sex. It is certainly mute about any sexual life of Jesus. Where it does speak of sex, the tone is negative. I think it fair to say, later developments in the church notwithstanding, that for the New Testament writers sex is not an important concern. Why not?

The first time I wrote about this, I argued that New Testament silence regarding Jesus' sexuality represented a kind of tacit desacralizing of sex (Driver 1965). Among divine and semidivine savior figures, especially in the Mediterranean and the Ancient Near East, Jesus was unusual in that his legend contained no stories of sexual activity. Neither were there any about his sexual asceticism. He was a savior figure who had nothing to do with sex one way or the other; and so, I proposed, sexuality might be seen by Christians as having been secularized, demythologized, while the ethical and soteriological meaning of the gospel was directed elsewhere. So interpreted, the gospels had dealt, by their very silence, the death blow to the religions of sexuality. I did realize that the sexlessness of Jesus posed a problem for the doctrine of Incarnation. An unsexual Jesus is only too likely to seem not truly human, leading to a latent if not overt Docetism in the church, as has surely been the case. However, I hoped that we might have a secularized view of sex without necessarily having a Docetic (i.e., not really human) Christ.

Today I think my earlier argument was naïve. It put too much weight on an argument from silence. Its hope for a truly human Christ who remained out of touch with human sexuality was wishful thinking, a rather desperate attempt to patch over a wide and deep problem. My answer to the question why the New Testament was so little concerned with sex was partly right but not right enough to avoid missing the point. The point missed, which today seems of utmost importance, is the New Testament's preoccupation with eschatology.

The New Testament is everywhere concerned with faith in Jesus as the avatar of a new age, the end of an old one. The texts were composed during the seventy or so years after Jesus' death in the belief that his return and the end of the old ways were imminent. In such a context, their near-silence about sex becomes easier to understand. So does the fact that the few sentences they do have are of a negative cast. The attitude toward sex, opaque and unclear though it be, is of a piece with New Testament ambivalence about, and basic disregard for, all the structures that sustain human society. One will look in vain for New Testament clarity about government, money, law (both sacred and secular), religion, family life, and so on. Except for St. Paul's discourses on "the Law," which are ambivalent in the extreme, none of these social realities gets much attention. Of course, one does not expect the New Testament to be systematic, but that is just the point. There is no reason to be systematic when the known world is about to disappear.

Trying to understand the New Testament attitude, I find help in the concepts of the anthropologist Victor Turner, who distinguishes between social structure and antistructure (Turner 1969; for further explication of this theory, see Chapter 8, below). Structure refers to those institutions, ranks, privileges, duties, role expectations, and so on by which a society maintains itself, gets necessary work performed, and commands discipline in times of crisis. Antistructure refers to special rituals and styles of life which express what Turner calls *communitas* — that is, communal life freed from duty and devoted to existence in mutual love. *Communitas* is the soul of society, violated more often than not by "realistic" necessity and human greed. Antistructures mock and transcend social structures to express the *communitas* living hidden and expectant in the heart of society.

The New Testament has scant interest in what Turner has defined as structure. Its attention is fastened upon *communitas*, and on the Messiah who will bring from God its antistructures. In the heavenly community, people will not marry. (It's not clear what they *will* do.) There they are neither male nor female, having been set "free." (It's not clear what they will look like.) There they will not have physical bodies, but instead what St. Paul calls "spiritual" bodies. (Usage forbids me to call them antibodies, although that is the idea, as we can detect when Paul speaks of them with privitive terms: *in*corruptible, *im*mortal, and so on.) There is to be no law in heaven, and yet the law will be everywhere fulfilled.

Christian communities in New Testament times, as far as we can glimpse them in its pages, are somewhere between structure and antistructure, between society and that *communitas* which Jesus called the kingdom of heaven. Wherever there is an idea or activity to express *communitas* rather clearly, the New Testament lights up in positive affirmation. The breaking of bread in the common meal is one of these (antistructure to the Pharisees' strict rules for ritualized eating, as well as to the routines and the privatism of most ordinary meals). So also the holding of "all things in common," the hymns, the abandonment of circumcision, Jesus' acts of healing on the Sabbath, his miracles, his acceptance of women, his aphorisms collected as a "sermon" on the Mount of Olives, and above all his subjection to structure when he died on the cross and his escape from it in resurrection.

New Testament Christians were counseled frequently to submit themselves to social structure: "Servants, be obedient to your masters" (Eph. 6:5; Tit. 2:9); "Wives, submit yourselves unto your husbands" (Eph. 5:22); "Render unto Caesar the things that are Caesar's" (Matt. 22:21), and so on. But they were also promised that all this would pass away soon. The days of structure were nearly over. Insofar as one had "the mind of Christ," they were as good as gone already.

Notably absent from New Testament thought about *communitas* is sexual abandon. This is frequently present in religious communities, leading to ideas (and often practices) of sexual freedom and orgy. There is evidence from the second century that some Christians went that way. One is amazed to find so little suggestion of it in the New Testament. The clearest hint is in a rebuke Paul sent to the church at Corinth: "It is reported commonly that there is fornication among you" (I Cor. 5:1). He was by no means pleased. The absence of sexual abandon as part of the New Testament picture of *communitas* is what prompted me in 1965 to say that the New Testament had desacralized sex, but then I had overlooked the eschatological expectation.

Whatever his involvement in, avoidance of, or attitude toward, sex may have been, the New Testament Jesus preached the imminent arrival of the *communitas* of God. After his death and resurrection, his followers preached that message and waited for that day. The end of oppressive social structures—indeed of *all* structure in Turner's sense of the term, the end of the "world" as they put it—was good news. Of course, it would not be good for those whose whole identities were invested in the structures, for they would lose all they had; but there was now time and reason for them to "repent," to turn away from present values toward those of God's coming kingdom by putting their faith in the Messiah Jesus. It is a measure of the New Testament Christians' passionate eschatological faith, their certainty that the new day was at hand, that a subject like sex is hardly worth mentioning. When it does come up (cf. Rom. 1:24–32), it is by way of speaking against all attachment to the ways of the world, for which Paul's word is "idolatry."

It is not for me, and I think not for anyone else, to turn the biblical Christ into something he wasn't. If we try to do him over so he will fit what we experience now, we will come to hate him. And if we repudate our own sexual experience because it does not fit what Jesus was, we shall hate ourselves. I myself have crossed over a line somewhere along the way and am no longer willing to think that my sexuality is sinful. I have come even further than that. I think that sexuality is positively necessary for loving God with a whole heart and loving our neighbors as ourselves. I am finding something holy in sexuality, as I was afraid to do in 1965, and this is leading me, as I then feared it would, to find good in many forms of sexual "irregularity." The further I go this way, the more the biblical Christ baffles and frustrates me. Trying to hold fast to him, I become angry. It's a little like Dietrich Bonhoeffer trying to hold fast to God "up above" until he realized, in prison, that he didn't *need* that God, that he could be a better Christian if he let God be absent. Letting go of God, Bonhoeffer found the more in Christ Jesus. I'm in a similar yet opposite position. I feel that God is more present than Jesus, more here and now and still to come than is Jesus. It's as if I have two masters and must hate the one if I am to love the other, for I can believe in a sexual God more honestly than I can believe in a sexual Jesus.

I imagine that I hear, in spite of his absence across the wide waters of time, the voice of Jesus. It says, "Do not hate me. Let me go." I hear in that, more than anything else, the voice of a friend. My friend is gone. My absent friend. My friend with whom I cannot live all the time. My friend from whom I once learned much but who knows little of the land I live in now. God knows more than he.

I must go my way and leave my friend to his. Very likely we shall one day meet again. What, I wonder, will he be like then? And what will I? In the meantime, now that I have permission to pursue my sexuality, where shall I go?

I write in the first-person singular, but I certainly do not believe that sex is solitary business. It is not really *my* sexuality that is the problem: it's *ours*. The sexual confusions of middle-class white America could be safely left to therapists if these confusions did not have so much to do with the world's injustice. A society cannot have a lot of religious confusion about sex running around and still hope to be clear about war, poverty, and greed. You can't have a war going on between the sexes, as we do so much of the time, or have an unjust sexist truce, as we had the day before yesterday, and pretend this has nothing to do with class conflict, racism, and tyranny. It was stupid of me ever to have thought that sex is a minor matter, either in religion or in social ethics. I might as well have said that it doesn't matter all that much if people have enough to eat. When I now take up the subject of emergent sexuality and Christ in present-future time, I am delving into a *social* question, and one of my first tasks is to show that the modern relegation of sex to the "private" sphere is a delusion dangerous to human survival and human justice.

There is so much to be said about how sex bears upon ethics and religion that I must choose only a little to say here. In one chapter of one book I cannot lay out a whole theology of sex, even if I knew how. I will have to stick close to my overall theme, which is that of an ethical christology for present-future time. The trinitarian discussion in the previous chapter leads to the major theme of this one: how to get beyond the dualisms so crippling in Christian thinking about sex. I will choose from a list of dualisms only two for discussion. One is the dichotomy between public and private sexuality. The other is the duality of genders, male and female. Important shifts are going on today with respect to both of these divisions, and they will affect what the churches can teach about God and Christ.

The Christian teachings on which I grew up are probably typical of that stream of Christianity which avoids the most puritanical attitudes about sex but finds little to put in their place. As I reflect upon these teachings nowadays, I am most struck by their dualistic assumptions. A person was either a virgin or was not. One was either married or single, either male or female, attracted always to the opposite sex or else had "gone wrong." One was either in love or not, and underlying all else was a division between sex and "higher things," almost equivalent to the fundamental differences between bad and good. As a "good son," I was expected to be virginal, avoiding sexual experience of every kind, until I was married, when it was assumed that I would at once become sexually virile and able to cope with any and all never-mentioned difficulties of the marriage bed. If I did not, that was my "personal problem."

The most positive legacy of my early sexual education from church and family was to connect sexuality with love. This ideal was stronger, or at least more often enunciated, in my Protestant milieu than the connection between sex and procreation, no doubt because my parents and teachers belonged to the first generation to enjoy the benefits of "artificial" methods of birth control, which I discovered they did make use of although they never spoke of it until long after I was married. They did speak of the importance of love between sexual (that is, married) partners. For this I am grateful. I was raised to view sex as having to do with deep feeling, and although I now think that is not a sufficient view of it, I believe it is a necessary component of a commendable sexual ethic. It is insufficient, naïve, and ultimately harmful only when it remains caught in a dualistic perspective, as it was in my training, from which I have subsequently had to extract it.

The problem with "love" as an ethical principle or as a factor in understanding oneself and others is that it is seldom, if ever, pure. To justify sexuality by the presence of love in it is to throw one into a very grey area, for love is not something like a water valve that may be either on or off. "Loving" and "unloving" do not form a very useful dichotomy, for in most experiences and certainly in most sexual relations the two are mixed in an ever-changing ratio. This is one reason the biblical Christ is so irrelevant to sexual life. He is taken to have been, or at least to represent, the "always loving." But life, as sexuality makes very clear, cannot be always loving. Rather, its most obvious characteristic is that it is always changing. The dynamic of growth and indescribable variety in a healthy sexual life renders it incapable of being adequately understood in dualistic terms.

Christianity has a particularly unfortunate way of viewing dualities because it also has a strong pull toward *monistic* thinking, the result of its religious belief in a sovereign God vs. not-God, or Good vs. Evil. When trinitarian thinking is weak, the idea of God as essentially unrelated to anything else, already perfect in goodness, becomes the idea of God immutable. Sexuality must then be associated with evil because it is variable, changing, and, in every sense of the word, relative. It is thought to need being "redeemed" by the presence of an unchanging love. Unfortunately for this point of view, love itself is variable. The more one loves, the more one is plunged into the vagaries of erotic life. This happens even to celibates, as the records of their fantasy life and the history of monasticism show.

Under what I may call monistic dualism, which is resistant to change, sexuality must either be seen as evil or lose all its meaning. In the days when Christianity found sex meaningful as the act of procreation, it linked sex with the dynamic of human life while adopting the view that if the link with childbearing were broken, sex would be evil. Now that the link *has* been broken by the advent of birth control and (even more) by the necessity to reduce the world's birthrate, it is imperative to find a new link between sex and the welfare of humanity. Otherwise, sex will become ever more meaningless and will be seen by Christians increasingly as evil (for which there will be much evidence in public debauchery) with consequent damage to mind, body, and community.

It is not hard to see why sex becomes mired in dualistic thinking. Where there is sexuality in biological life, there is male and female. As obvious as day and night, this truism becomes just as pervasive as day and night in myth, psychology, theory, and law. What would we know of ourselves if we did not "know" the duality of the sexes? Not much, indeed; but if this is all we know, we know little.

Strong in its hold upon human minds, the duality of the sexes attracts, if it does not spawn, a number of other dualisms, which seem to reinforce each other. Notable among these are spirit/flesh, fidelity/infidelity, monogamy/promiscuity, work/pleasure, marriage/divorce, and (in modern times) private/public. The lack of a vigorous Christian sexual ethic in our time is largely due to obsession with these dualisms. We need a christology which can assist Christian imagination to transcend them. Let the reader understand that I regard the dualities as real, but not real enough for the best ethical decisions.

The dualisms I have mentioned run parallel to one another and can be grouped as follows:

male	female
spirit	flesh
fidelity	infidelity
work	pleasure
monogamy	promiscuity

marriage	divorce
private	public
good	evil

As with all dualisms, the terms in any one pair may occasionally be turned around. The concepts in the left-hand column are conventionally understood as "better" than those in the right. However, there is often a minority who protest this by inverting the values. Flesh becomes "better" than spirit, female superior to male, promiscuity more "liberated" than monogamy, and so on.

There is also protest, which I share, against the stereotypes. It is certainly stereotypical thinking to link female with flesh and infidelity while associating male with spirit and constancy, as is done especially in the Christian religion. One gets tired of these cliches. They do not correspond to experience, not even when they are turned upside down. It will do no good, however, to ignore them.

Two entries on my list of dualisms may help us think:

| marriage | divorce |
| private | public |

Why do I not think of marriage as public, divorce as private? One gets married in church, sends out invitations, has a celebration. If divorce comes, one sneaks off to a lawyer, sends out no announcements, hopes not many people will notice. We boast of our marriages and try to hide our divorces, which we regard as failures.

Nonetheless, the modern split between public and private has put marriage in the private sphere, divorce in the public. The reason is simple: marriage, having become centered on sex, is thought to be none of the public's business. It is regarded as a contract between two "private individuals." Although the couple's friends, families, and even employers may try to butt in, the couple are essentially on their own.

When couples arrive requesting me to officiate at their wedding, I have taken to asking them if they have any good reason to marry, since I assume these days that they can have sex and even live together "without benefit of clergy," as the old phrase put it. Their usual answer is that they love each other, and I point out that no license is required for that. I even point out that there is a respected, if half-forgotten, tradition of "common-law marriage," which recognizes a couple's love and fidelity and common right to property without there having been a marriage ceremony. They usually say something then about the importance to them of a ritual (a subject I shall address in the next chapter), and I inquire what they understand as the subject or meaning of a wedding ritual. Few have thought about this, since the ritual is simply "there" for the asking. I then say that a marriage contract, although it is undertaken by two people in their own right, is nevertheless a contract acknowledging the vested interest of *other* people in this particular relationship, its quality and its endurance. These "others" may include the couple's children (born or unborn at present), parents, other relatives, and friends. Always involved, say I, is society, whose interest is established by a law requiring a marriage license. And then, since they have come to me, the church has an interest, and so does God. If they want to be married, they should realize that marriage is a public matter involving family, society, and religious community. It is not merely or essentially a private agreement to stay together, which in any case they have already made.

I wish I had movies of the faces of the couples to whom I have said these things. Their looks pass gradually from incomprehension to disappointment. If they decide nonetheless to go through with the ceremony, they put on a face of affable compliance. After all, once the wedding is over, they can do and think as they please. Or so they imagine. Like Romeo and Juliet, they are prepared to leave their elders' opinions behind. Like those famous lovers, they take it for granted that marriage is a private matter between themselves only, society be damned. Marriage means whatever they will have it mean, and the public dimension of it is simply part of the hassle of living. I have often been seduced by their faith in what they mean to each other, but I think I have finally grown immune, and I have sworn off performing weddings. The myth of the privacy of marriage comes to too much grief when confronted by public realities, which storm in with terrible force as soon as the marriage shows signs of strain. A couple may have a big wedding, but the marriage is held to be a secret of the bedroom, until it ends in public court.

In our society, marriage is turned into a "personal" commitment,

and divorce is a public statistic. The role of the churches is especially indicative. They bless marriage as a union of two souls, and they
ignore divorce as they ignore the weather. In the eyes of the
churches, divorce is as secular as marriage is holy. Its causes are
consigned to "things as they are," while marriage is still regarded as
a grace of God. The day I hear that divorces are blessed in church I
will know that marriage has come out of the closet.

In the preceding chapter, on trinitarian thinking, I referred to
the way in which the idea of personhood has become privatized in
modern societies, producing a split in our minds between the personal and the public. I maintained that this diminution in the
meaning of "personal" by its divorce from "public" is evidence of a
decline in trinitarian thinking, from which the European tradition
had first learned the concepts of person and personhood. Now I
may point out that one of the worst effects of this bifurcation has
been a loss of the public meaning of sex. Since the phrase "public
meaning of sex" may itself seem strange to modern readers, I must
explain what I think is going on.

Contrary to popular opinion, sexuality in our culture has gone
private. I do not, of course, mean that sex is not on public display
and is not the subject of endless discussion: quite the opposite. I
mean that sex has lost its public or commonly shared *meaning*, that
what it does or should mean has been relegated to the privacy of individuals and their "personal relationships." The more public becomes the display of sex, the literature of sex, and its availability in
pictures, words, and flesh, the more its communal meaning departs
from public view, taking refuge in the curtained bedroom or the
privacy of individuals' minds. It is like food in the supermarket: so
much is available (for a price) and in such variety (for those willing
to look around) that one either ends up getting what everyone else
seems to be getting or else cultivates an individual taste. Virtually
gone are the days when food had a public meaning derived from the
fact of shared dependence upon, and enjoyment of, the weekly
rhythms of the local baker and the seasonal rhythms of the neigh-
borhood greengrocer. Sexuality has experienced a similar fate.
Knowledge of when is the right time for sex, with whom, and for
what purpose has been vitiated in our mass-production society. Sex
is now everywhere all the time, and so its meaningfulness has either

evaporated or taken shelter in "private understandings" and in enclaves such as families and small religious groups.

In his *History of Sexuality* (1978) Michel Foucault has reasoned that the modern increase of talk and published information about sex has not resulted in an increase of sexual freedom. He holds instead that our sexuality is ever more subject to control and regulation by a moot collaboration between government and sexual research. He thinks this process began in confessional booths in the seventeenth century and was later secularized. Be that as it may, the conjecture is quite compatible with what I refer to as sexuality's loss of public meaning. When meaningfulness retreats to the private sphere, the public domain is the more easily manipulated. Conversely, manipulation of the public domain by powerful institutions forces the retreat of personal meanings into privacy. The churches have abetted this from both sides. As public institutions they have had little to say in recent times about what sex means, yet they have done everything they could to control and manage sexual behavior, sexual laws, sexual communication, and so on. Meanwhile, on the private front, they have encouraged an ideology of sex as meaningful only within the parameters of a circle drawn around the couple. Christian ideology concerning the privacy of sex, like its other sexual opinions, becomes especially clear when the subject is homosexuality.

Nearly twenty years ago, the Quakers in England issued a statement on homosexuality in which they said that Christians should not condemn, and the state should not interfere with, sexual acts committed between consenting adults in private. This has become the prevailing liberal view, Christian and otherwise. Even those conservative Christians in the United States who think the churches should condemn all homosexual acts do not ask the state to interfere as long as the acts are private. The antigay campaign of Anita Bryant, for example, was directed against the public (civil) rights of avowed homosexuals, while the controversy over the churches' ordination of homosexuals is centered upon public profession, not private behavior, it being an open secret that male homosexuals have been ordained throughout Christian history provided they did not make their inclinations public. There is a tacit understanding that what people do about sex in private is nobody else's business.

I was asked to write a review (Driver 1963) of the Quaker statement. While I applauded the charity and lack of fanaticism in the
document, I took issue with its reasoning. I said that there is no
such thing as private sexuality: all sex, even that behind closed
doors, is of a public character and bears upon the public weal. For
this reason I appealed for the recovery of a sense of humor about
sex. I felt that the Quakers, like most latter-day Christians, most
psychologists, and certainly judges and lawmakers, had fallen into
taking sex so "seriously" that they thought it immoral to laugh at it.
Indeed, on the day my article was published a theological colleague
reprimanded me on the street, saying that a Christian should "never
make sex the object of humor"! Such an attitude, admittedly extreme in that particular man, is widespread among pious folk and
shows the split we have come to between public and private sexuality. Sexual humor is a way of making sex public and of inducing
communal understandings about it. To be long-faced about sex is
to imply that the subject really ought not to come up and can be
made socially (or religiously) acceptable only by great seriousness. I
argued for more sexual humor and less separation between public
and private in sexual ethics.

Whenever I tell students there is no such thing as private sex, they
are shocked. Unless they come from rural traditions, their upbring-
ing has not prepared them for such an idea. The first thing to enter
their heads when I say it is probably masturbation, or some love affair they dream of, or a recent sexual connection they have made,
all of which they have learned to regard as "nobody's business." I
hasten to explain to them that I do not mean they should tell everybody what they are doing. Public confession is not the same as
public meaning. I mean that sexual secrecy is like religious secrecy:
its meaning and value lie not in the secrecy but in the effect upon
one's communal life. For example, when a person withdraws to a
secluded place to masturbate, the privacy of the act is defined by its
relation to some "public" from which it is secluded: privacy is
always privacy *from*. There are people who will masturbate only in
the dark because they seek privacy from all possible seeing, including their own. Or else the darkness helps them to imagine some
particular spectator (and not others) whose gaze they desire. We are
social creatures even in our privacy and individualism.

Not only do our fantasies of sexual desire arise from social experience, they also feed it. Sexual life is, if I may so put it, a kind of digestive process. (The linkage between sex and food is very close, and I shall refer to it more than once.) Through sexual or erotic appetite, physical contact, and fantasy we "ingest" a portion of our social life. During extended fantasy and other sexual pleasures we "digest" this material. It passes through deep recesses of tissue and consciousness, mixed there with our life "blood." When the session is over, we have, in whole or in part, for better or worse, "metabolized" the sexual experience, returning to the public world not quite the same as before. Sexual contact, fantasy, and intercourse are as necessary to public life as are food, clothing, and shelter. In both types of need, public and private overlap, while physical and spiritual converge. Christian conscience is used to discerning the spiritual dimension of food, which is manifest in the eucharistic meal and in the injunction to feed the hungry; but Christian conscience has not discerned the spiritual dimension of sex resident in the fact that it is a fundamental human need, like food, inseparable from our modes of relating to one another for good or ill.

Regarding both food and sex (not to mention shelter and clothing), the paramount ethical challenge of our time is to overcome an outdated and now pernicious ethic of "private property."

As capitalism has made a fetish of private property, so has it also made the privacy of sex into something sacrosanct. What this accomplishes is to leave the public sphere vacant of all religious meaning so that it is open for plunder by that very same capitalism. A man's home may be his castle, but that does not prevent foreclosure on the mortgage or slum landlords letting apartment houses decay to increase their profit. One face of "private property" may be a trimmed lawn in front of the home of a settled family, but the other face is exploitation of those who cannot afford the property that makes such privacy possible. Similarly, one face of sexual privacy may be the faithful couple who love each other tenderly at night, but the other is the sex industry, as G. B. Shaw pointed out long ago in the play *Widower's Houses.* The ideology of capitalism is to prevent our seeing that its two faces are connected, just as the ideology of the churches is to have us think that they are responsible for marriage and not divorce, for spirit and not flesh, for hetero-sexuality and not homosexuality, for monogamy and not promiscuity, for a male Christ and not a female.

Privatization of sexual *meaning* alongside public display of sexual *facts* has been caused partly by industrial capitalism and partly by Christian teaching. Christianity has tended to perpetuate a sexual ethic ever more anachronistic, increasingly irrelevant to public life. Failing to address the public meaning of sex in adequate social, let alone spiritual, terms, it has left a vacuum to be filled by merchants.

In the main, as is well known, Christianity has regarded sex as a necessary evil. The biblical Christ was taken to have been celibate. By the second century, women were being excluded from Christian ministry, which eventually became both male and celibate. Contrary to the teaching of the Old Testament and Judaism, sexuality became wedded to sin. The only justification the church fathers found for sex was the necessity of procreation. "I praise marriage and wedlock," said St. Jerome, "but only because they beget celibates" (quoted in Nelson 1978, p. 52).

However negative the idea of "sex for procreation only" may sound today, we should remember that it once gave to sexuality a definite public meaning, widely understood in terms of a theory of natural law. The whole of one's sexual life, whether it was virtuous or sinful, could be interpreted by reference to its aim of replenish-ing the species. Even celibacy gained meaning from this view, for it enabled the priest to become a spiritual "father." In spite of Christianity's negative view of all sexual acts, as it spread across Europe it made common cause with folk wisdom to understand sex as vital to the public welfare. At its height in the Middle Ages, Christianity was the religion of a very lusty culture, its pervasive en-joyment of sex manifest in literature from the courtly love poets to Chaucer. In the eleventh and twelfth centuries there was even a flourishing "gay" subculture, tolerated by the church at large and extolled in the writings of many clerics (Boswell 1980). Like the tra-dition of courtly love, however, with which it was contemporane-ous, this movement could not long survive the dominant idea that the only good of sex lay in procreation. In the latter twelfth and thirteenth centuries, under a militant papacy and the increasing power of national governments, it was stamped out, along with the heterosexual marriages of priests (Boswell 1980 and Barstow 1979).

Monasticism aside (and after the takeover of the papacy by monks in the eleventh century it could not be left aside), the sexual ethic of medieval Christianity was that of an agrarian people not far removed from tribal consciousness. By agrarian, I mean people whose food and clothing are locally produced, mostly on the land occupied by one's family. By tribal, I mean a social organization based upon extended families and a network of marriages and other personal ties. Such were the antecedents of feudalism, out of which grew European royalty. One has only to think of the fateful importance of Henry VIII's determination to sire a son to get a sense of how public was the meaning of sex up to the middle of the sixteenth century.

Capitalism, democracy, and industrialism have gradually removed the meaning of sex from public life. Tribal agrarian organization and its mentality are atavistic oddities now. The major step in the privatization of sex has been the transformation of the family from a producing unit of the economy into a consuming unit, which is principally the result of the industrial revolution and its need of mobile, anonymous labor. Modern technology, an offspring of industrialization, invented devices for birth control, just in time (perhaps) to ward off a catastrophic rise in population. Today the world as a whole and most nations within it have more people than are needed, and overpopulation of the globe is a serious danger. The public justification of sex as the means of procreation has been shattered.

Today, sex is in need of new meaning capable of being shared by the public and having clear value for the life of society. This need the churches have not clearly seen, or perhaps have not wanted to face. When they do not continue to insist that the meaning of sex is on the one hand sin and on the other babies, they encourage an ideology of privatism, looking for ways to bless an essentially private meaning of sex as the expression of love between husband and wife. (For a good review of these developments and controversies in the Roman Catholic church, see The Catholic Theological Society of America 1977.) All forms of sex outside this intensely private one are either condemned or merely tolerated.

Sexuality cannot be contained within the private sphere. Not only is it too strong a biological drive, its potential meaning is too great. I see people in modern society as knowing that sex should have meaning beyond the privacy of couples but little imagining what that meaning may be. They pick up partners, swap mates, hold orgies, make skin-flicks, marry repeatedly, and engage in all manner of sexual experimentation in the vague hope that a transcendent meaning will emerge. Most people in our society, even the stay-at-homes, seem to be caught up in this search. If we are honest about it, we will see that the biblical Christ is here of no direct help at all, unless we decide, as the Roman church would still like us to do, that the most meaningful sexual life is celibate and the next-best is propagation.

In this regard, James B. Nelson's *Embodiment* (1978) is very instructive, since it is the only book I know to have seen the need for a Christian "sexual theology" and not simply a "sexual ethic" derived from a theology worked out on other terms. He writes:

> For too long the bulk of Christian reflection about sexuality has asked an essentially one-directional question: what does Christian faith have to say about our lives as sexual beings? Now we are beginning to realize that the enterprise must be a genuinely two-directional affair. The first question is essential, and we must continue unfailingly to press it. But at the same time it must be joined by, indeed interwoven with, a companion query: what does our experience as sexual human beings mean for the way in which we understand and attempt to live out the faith? (pp. 9f.)

I hope that *Embodiment* will be very widely read. With what it has to say about sexuality I have very little disagreement and much enthusiasm. However, it fails to press its theological questions far enough to achieve the intended "sexual theology." Although its statements about God are helpful, it does not face up to christological issues nor have much to say about Spirit. Falling short of christological and trinitarian reasoning, its theology is unable to break out of the dualisms in Christian thinking about sex which Nelson correctly sees as the heart of the problem.

In my third chapter, on the critique of Christ as center, model, and norm, I cited in disagreement one portion of an article published by Nelson shortly before *Embodiment* (see above, pp. 52f.). I said that a statement in the article declaring Jesus Christ to be the "normative model" of Nelson's thinking about sex is without substance. The statement does not occur in his book, but he does throughout imply that his proposed revisions of Christian teaching about sex suggest no change in Christ or God. Nelson seems to accept the eternal sameness of these, relegating change to human culture, experience, and understanding. With this, as the foregoing chapters make clear, I do not agree. I take it that a genuine conflict exists between the biblical Christ and our best contemporary understandings of reality.

The route I suggest for reenvisioning Christ as a figure who belongs now (as not before) to the human sexual community is through a trinitarian understanding of sexual dualisms. That is to say, we might start with our experiences of the polarized dualities in sexual life and pursue their meaning in the context of divine spirit, becoming informed thereby as to the Christ whom we expect in present-future time. This means viewing the Christian community as a community of christic expectation, to which the memory of Christ past, while not rubbed out, is subordinate. The dualities of the sexual, as of other, aspects of life help to define the content of any christic expectation, but in a trinitarian context they do not freeze it.

It is helpful to distinguish three types of thinking about dualities in life: the "cosmic" dualism of ancient Greek thought, the "monistic" dualism of much Christian thinking, and the "relative" dualism of trinitarian thought. "Cosmic" dualism is the idea that the opposing forces and qualities of life are part of a single, unified whole known to Greek philosophy as the "cosmos." Cosmic dualism results from a tension between polytheism and monotheism. As polytheists, the Greeks could value the linkage, overlap, and energy potential between opposites. Ares (war) and Aphrodite (sexual love) could be seen as opposites, while their affinity could be expressed in stories of their marital union. The battles, connivings, and love affairs of all the Greek gods are representations of the ways in which the important forces of life, often polarized, relate to one another. The pantheon itself represents the idea that all the forces belong to a single divine totality. The principle of Greek morality, then, was to give everything its due, finding a proper "moira" (share or portion) for the bad as well as the good, the Dionysian as well as the Apollonian, and so on. A similar tension between many opposing gods (read "forces" or "principles") and a wholistic unity of them (a monotheistic tendency) is to be found in many of the world's religions, notably in Africa. The same tension is the basis of the psychology of Carl Jung, which envisions the self as a kind of cosmic whole made up of antagonistic but potentially harmonious components, therapy becoming a kind of worship of the whole, in which each component is given due homage by the conscious self.

"Monistic" dualism is the result of a monotheism which ascribes to God alone a total and perfect goodness. When this is done, the dualities of life become a problem, for it is difficult, if not impossible, to see how a unitary God of perfect goodness can be the author of a creation that is, in so many ways, divided against itself. If all results from One, and if that One is good, how is it that the world is composed of forces, principles, and values that are in opposition to each other? This question causes absolute monotheism ever and again to assimilate all dualities into a single contrast between Good and Evil. In every duality a good and a bad side are then seen. Essentially there is thought to be only one conflict—God overcoming everything that is not God. Although this leaves "the problem of Evil" unresolved, it protects the idea that "in himself" God is perfect and good. What it loses, and this is why Christianity is in such ethical trouble today, is the ability to discern that there are virtues in vices and that all moral decisions have to do not with absolute but with relative judgments. When this ethical relativity *is* discerned, as, for example, in the writings of Reinhold Niebuhr, it is taken as evidence of "the Fall."

The relative or radical trinitarian thinking which I advanced in the previous chapter is an altered version of cosmic dualism, altered by modern historical thinking, by theories of relativity, and by the Christian doctrine of Trinity. Like cosmic dualism, it views the dualities of life as parts of a divine whole, placing great value on their variety, subtlety, and power. However, it differs from cosmic dualism in thinking that the cosmic whole is not finite and may not be envisioned as having, either now or later, a finished boundary. Its cosmos is open, like a radiational field, not closed like a perfect circle. Therefore, time and unbounded energy play here a much more positive role than in cosmic dualism, displacing the preeminent value which the Greeks placed upon perfection of form. In its break with the idea of God's perfection and timelessness, radical trinitarian thought is similar to process theology, but it differs in not entertaining the idea of a "primordial nature" of God which is absolute and a "consequential nature" of God which is finite and moving processively to perfection along with the finite world. If radical trinitarianism is less static than cosmic dualism, it is less linear than the Hegelian dialectic and the Whiteheadian idea of process. When confronted with any pair of opposites, therefore, it asks neither what complete whole they belong to nor to what "end" they point. Instead it asks what good may be expected to emerge from their creative interaction.

The ethic of radical trinitarian thought focuses upon emergent good in present-future time. It is concerned with the creative possibilities of relationships, whether these be relations among persons or among principles and forces. It regards every duality, including but not limited to the duality of two persons, as fraught with energy that is either open to the infinite field of God's spirit or is closed explosively against it. Even this either/or, however, is relative, because no duality, like no entity, is absolute. Every duality, being a kind of relation, exists in the "more" of its potential field. This said, I return to the split between public and private sexuality and then to the duality of male and female.

Among the polarities which characterize the structure of life, Paul Tillich used to speak of "individuation and participation" (Tillich 1951, pp. 174–178). It is often assumed, and Tillich himself leaves the impression, that sexuality pulls us toward participation, while our individuation inclines toward more solitary pursuits. It is more accurate, however, to see that sex includes both sides of the polarity and that this is one reason why the division between public and private is so heavily charged with sexual meaning. Insofar as it has to do with individuation, sex moves toward privacy, including the privacy of the couple; but insofar as it has to do with participation, sex moves toward being public. Christianity's emphasis on the individual soul's transactions with its unitary God has led to the exaltation of sexual privacy as a good and the denigration of

public sexuality as evil, with the consequent loss of the public meaning of sex which I have already pointed out. In other words, the
monistic dualism in which Christianity ensconces itself has robbed it
of the ability to foster a communal dimension of sex, cultivating
instead a kind of sexual participation limited to the privacy of the
couple. The more communal aims of sexuality, far from disappear-
ing, have had to express themselves in illicit and secularized forms
which the churches have been obliged to regard as vices. It is thus
not surprising to find today a resurgence of non-Christian religions — witchcraft, for example — that include awareness of the
sacrality of communal sex alongside the private.

Religious forms of communal sex in biblical times, severely condemned by both Judaism and Christianity, were labeled "prostitu-
tion." The name is misleading, since it suggests a commercial
motive. The practices did in time become commercialized, just as
Jesus found the temple at Jerusalem commercialized in other ways
by "money-changers"; but the original motive for treating sexual
intercourse as an act of communal worship was neither greed nor
mere lust. It was public recognition of sexuality as sacred — not
sacred in its privacy, not sacred as a symbol of one's secret unity
with a spouse or with God, but as a spiritual force belonging to the
public welfare. Fertility of crops, animals, and humans was only
one part of that welfare. Closer to the heart of it was ecstasy, which
was sought in group dancing as well as anonymous sex. The locus of
religion being a communal rather than a merely private transaction
with God, ecstasy was both a personal and a communal renewal of
life. The practices were a kind of "ritualized promiscuity."

It would be artificial and counterproductive for Christian
churches to introduce ritualized promiscuity into their life, and this
is certainly not my point. It is to my point to say that the churches
should recognize in the occurrence of promiscuity a drive toward
the social meaning of eroticism. Given our theology of a unitary
God and our ethos of private property, communal sex looks like
self-indulgence, lack of principle, and thievery. It may look very
different, however, if we perceive that public and private are two
valid sexual principles encountering each other in an infinite or
spiritual field. As privacy addresses the need of society for family
structures, sexual boundaries, and clear responsibilities,

promiscuity addresses the need for sharing, abandon, and the spiritually anonymous. The religious meaning of both the private and the public derives from their contextual grounding in the infinite Spirit of God.

Tillich (1963) spoke of the church as "the Spiritual Community." As such, we may see it as the home of both the monogamous and promiscuous, not because the church is "tolerant" and "forgiving," but because each group is in spiritual need of the other. To use an old phrase, each "bears witness" to the other, for it is in their mutual recognition of value that they both become aware of the field of dynamic holiness giving meaning to what they do. The monogamous and the promiscuous are not, all said and done, two different groups. Each group and each individual is, in varying ratio, both.

It has been the merit of Carl Jung, referred to above, to have made many modern Christians aware of the dualities of value within us, interpreting psychological and spiritual growth as the gradual acceptance and harmonization of inner polarities by the conscious self. I have already indicated that Jung's position is like that of "cosmic" dualism. Another difference between my thought and his lies in the split he imagines between inner and outer reality. Whereas Jungian thought is introverted and concentrates on the integration of self, I hold that Christianity is properly extroverted and concentrates on the just integration of society. Whereas Jung inclined toward the idea that the archetypal contents of the psyche are transhistorical and permanent, I believe that ideas, images, and even archetypes (if such there be) are historical in origin and are to be seen as having only relative stability within the dynamic field of trinitarian encounter among God, humanity, and world. The value of recognizing sexual dualities is not merely the prudent one of learning to give everything its due: it is the spiritual one of discerning the source of meaning in the potential for change. Wherever the knowledge of good and evil is too sure, and wherever certain principles, dualities, or archetypes are regarded as permanent, the spirit of God is denied.

The worldwide crisis in relations between women and men today, which is leading to a crisis in the churches regarding christological doctrine, is closely related to the duality of public and private I have been discussing. The uneasy truce between men and women which is now coming apart was based upon male dominance of the public world and female confinement to the private. I well remember my mother's belief, when I was young, that if a woman's name was in the newspaper anywhere except the "society" page, which dealt with weddings, births, and parties, it meant something was wrong. The women's movement is the assertion of women's right to public responsibility and status, which entails the right of women to self-determination. Insofar as women do the work of childbirth and nurture, feminism would show these as belonging to the public sphere, with a consequent loosening of the tight boundaries that have been erected around "the family" to protect its privacy. Care of children would become a more public responsibility, shared by men as well as women, and an anonymous or public parenthood would become more valuable than is possible under the sway of patriarchy.

The patriarchal idea of family is bloodline. This meaning of family was taken over by the Christian churches, who became so wedded to it that they have been resistant to recent changes in family structures. For example, a growing number of unmarried people are today clamoring to become foster parents: single men, single women, homosexual couples of both sexes, divorced people, and unmarried couples who do not want to add to the population but do want to nurture children already here. A large number of these people are sexual "sinners," and the majority of church people oppose their taking on family responsibilities. A Gallup poll conducted in 1978-1979 found that 84 percent of people who attend church in the United States answered "no" when asked whether homosexuals should be allowed to adopt children. The same poll found that the population as a whole answered "yes" to the same question by 87 percent (Princeton Religion Research Center 1979, pp. 103f.). These figures can only mean that church people believe in the badness of homosexuality more than in the need of homeless children to be adopted. However, if a homosexual actually fathers or gives birth to a child, the issue does not come up.

Idolization of family as bloodline through heterosexual union encourages attitudes that are racist, sexist, homophobic, proprietary, and cruel. The churches have played into these attitudes by depicting Christ as the "only begotten" son of God through the womb of a virginal mother.

Men, not women, have insisted on bloodline. To be sure, in response to male demand, women have taken up the theme. Internalizing the male-centered value of feminine "purity" (another word for privacy), women have sought to demonstrate how dutiful and faithful they are; but purity of bloodline, and therefore female chastity, is a patriarchal value. Unlike men, women have never been in any doubt that whatever children are born come from their loins. They have thus had a more public, less possessive, sense of parenthood than men.

The story of Jesus' "virgin birth" (Matt. 1:1-25) is instructive in its ambiguity about fatherhood. Matthew traces the bloodline of Jesus through Joseph back to King David. However, Joseph is then said not to be the father of Jesus. The story says Mary became pregnant before she and Joseph "came together," which gave rise to rumors of her promiscuity. This detail hints at the idea that Jesus' father was anonymous (cf. J. A. T. Robinson 1973, pp. 57ff.). Jesus would be, so to speak, a child of the streets or the fields, the same idea conveyed later by his birth in a stable, still later by the Son of Man having "nowhere to lay his head" (Matt. 8:20), and eventually his crucifixion between two nameless thieves. One connotation of "Son of Man" is son of nobody in particular, therefore the son of the race, a wandering stranger belonging to no one and thus to all. In patriarchal culture, to be "homeless" is not to lack a mother but to have no father, since the father, and not the mother, defines one's place in the world.

The idea that Jesus had no father is unacceptable in patriarchal culture. Matthew, having dropped such a hint, proceeds to tell how God became the father of Jesus, impregnating Mary by miracle. The story hovers between seeing Jesus as the fatherless child of humanity in general and a prince whose father is the king of heaven. The latter takes precedence, as in all fairy tales, and the Son of God begotten of the Father became the centerpiece of Christian patriarchy. There he will remain in past glory as long as the church remains patriarchal.

In patrilinear societies the responsibility of the father is to en-

gender the child and bestow identity upon it. Various other responsibilities may go along with these, but they may be delegated if necessary, as engenderment and identity bestowal may not. The
mother's responsibility, by contrast, is to nurture the father's child.
Her relation to it is "provisional": she provides for the child at the
pleasure of its father. Thus it comes about that the nurturing activi-
ties of everyone, female or male, are regarded as "feminine" and as
subordinate to the more "manly" function of bestowing identity.

Carried over into Christian theology, these patrilinear assumptions have meant that although all humans are "of woman
born"—that is, of the earth and of humanity generally—identity
comes from God the Father. In that case, the function of Christ as
the "eternal Son of God" is to restore to those born of women their
true inheritance from God above. Confessing "God the Father
Almighty . . . and Jesus Christ His only son," people become
"legitimate." In Evangelical parlance, they are "born again." In
more classical theological language, they are "redeemed." In the
language of that beautiful yet most sexist of Jesus' parables, they
have "come home" to their Father.

If the churches were to turn from Christ past to Christ present-
future in order to affirm the equality of women and men, Christian
identity would break loose from dependence on God the Father and
Christ, his Son. In fact, identity would cease to be a religious concern. It would be replaced by collaboration with God in the *nurture*
of life. Christ would not be the Son of God bringing all people home
to God by "justification." That was the job of the patrilinear Christ
of our past and Christians should regard it as a work completed.
Christ future is a human agent aware of coresponsibility with God
in the creative preservation of life. That awareness, and the political work necessary to put it into action, is the aim of Christian
feminism. It requires the emergence of autonomous womanhood,
for it is not the work of slaves, subordinates, or second-class status of
any kind.

The root meaning of the word "virgin" had nothing to do with
sexual innocence. It denoted only the innocence of having been sub-
jugated. It came later to denote sexual purity when fathers insisted
that their daughters be free of sex to make them more attractive to
a potential husband and master. Virginity as sexual innocence is a

concept developed to enhance and extend the proprietary interests of men. "The significance of the term 'virgin,' " Penelope Washbourn has written with respect to the word's ancient usage, "lies in its contrast to 'married.' In primitive times a woman was the property of her husband, having been bought from her father. As a virgin, however, she belongs to herself—she is 'one-in-herself!' " . . . The quality of virginity persists in spite of sexual experience, child bearing, or age" (Washbourn 1972, p. 98).

Unlike Washbourn (1972, p. 103), I do not see that Jesus' mother Mary is depicted in scripture or tradition as a virgin in the same sense as Washbourn's own sentences quoted above so well convey. Perhaps Matthew (1:23) cited the reference to a virgin in Isaiah 62:5 simply to mean that Mary was unmarried when Jesus was conceived, but this is not likely because the point of his narrative is to establish the parentage of Jesus and the means of his conception. Although Matthew's text is ambiguous, it paved the way for later tradition's emphasis on Mary's virginity in the debased sense of that word, a woman who had not had sexual intercourse. In any case, the Bible has no interest in who Mary was or what she did in her own right. She is depicted as the "vessel" of the will of a most definitely male God, who seems to select her as one who is innocent not only of sex but of everything else.

The doctrine of Jesus' "virgin birth," from which I do not think it is possible to separate the biblical Christ, must be seen as corollary to the doctrine of God's creation *ex nihilo*. In both, God creates by working "his" will upon *nothing*. The "virgin birth" makes explicit that same regard of woman as "nothing" which is implicit in the *creatio ex nihilo*. Both doctrines rest upon the ancient sexist view that the male parent (creator) supplies all that is real (the *identity*) in the offspring. Starting with nothing, God is supposed to have created the world entirely out of "his" own will and Word. The "formless void" of Genesis 1:1 is here taken as nothing at all, no "other" with which God has to come to any terms or which makes any contribution to the created result. The "formless void" is thus like an "empty" woman upon whom the Lord works his wonders. This is not the most apt reading of Genesis 1, but it is the reading required by *creatio ex nihilo*. In the "virgin birth" of Jesus, God again works "his" wonder upon a woman who is "nothing." Unlike

Joseph, she has no history. Her will is totally compliant to the an-
nunciating angel. Later she observes what happens and "stores"
things in her heart. As a result of this total compliance she is
eventually elevated to be the "Queen of Heaven," where she can
intercede on behalf of those who call upon her, but never in her
whole story does she do anything in her own right, unless it be to
utter the poem called The Magnificat, in which her soul, as her
womb had done, "magnifies the Lord."

The myth of the all-male male—that is, the male beholden to
nothing that is not male—saturates the figure of Christ past. It does
so in spite of those touches in the gospels, surely authentically historical, which show Jesus' attitudes to have been far less sexist than
most of his culture. It was not the feminist Jesus who became Christ,
the center of all things. To state the matter conversely, it was not a
feminine Logos who was in Jesus made flesh. That is why Christian
feminism must necessarily have a quarrel with Christ past and with
all theological doctrine bound to that figure and his Father. This
throws up a watershed for feminists. We must decide whether
Christian doctrine can be freed from the hold of Christ past upon it
while still remaining Christian. If so, a Christian feminism is possible. If not, one has to bind the feet of one's feminism to conform it
to Christ past, or else to leave the church.

There are many motifs in feminism, many varieties of it. I focus
the issue as I see it: the possibility of a *christological* affirmation of
female autonomy. I have reached the conclusion that this is not possible as long as the biblical Christ is regarded as final, decisive,
eternal, or central.

Autonomous womanhood is not a memory: it is an expectation.
Except for a sentence or two by Paul in the context of eschatological
abolition of all social structure, the New Testament contains no
promise of women's autonomy. This expectation, while it is not
without precedent in history, is nevertheless fundamentally *new* as a
historical movement, made so not by Christian impetus but by
changed patterns of work, reproduction, and communication in the
modern world. It is not the old Christ who can meet this expectation in the christic form of God's infinite commitment to finitude.
For that, we have to look in present-future time, informed but not
governed by our reflections upon the past.

In my mind's eye, and in many others' too, there is a vision of relation between women and women, women and men, men and men. The vision is hardest to bring to focus when the partners are women and men, and it is here that radical trinitarian thought may be of most help. The vision itself was memorably stated by Marlo Thomas in a newspaper article (*The New York Times*, April 19, 1978). She wrote of herself and other women learning "to look directly into the eyes of men from whom you want *nothing* — except a serious conversation." This "innocent" vision has everything to do with sexuality, as I trust may be clear. It does not envision the denial of sex for the sake of a "better" transaction but the affirmation of equality for the sake of a more wholehearted sexuality. To want "nothing except conversation" is not necessarily to exclude sex but to be free of the partner's sexual demand, including the projection of that demand onto oneself as a seductress and a sex object.

The equality of male and female is a religious expectation, although Marlo Thomas and many other feminists may not recognize it as such. I call it religious because it transcends past and present history and is not adequately addressed by a rational theory of innate or even postulated equality between the sexes. It is born of awareness that there is something sacred not about the fact or the principle but about the *ethic* of an I-Thou encounter. The awesomeness of the experience of looking deeply into the eyes of another person and recognizing there a self equal in power and need to one's own is the awareness that our mutual recognition is a constellation of energy within a relational field of infinite power and meaning. It is holy. The awareness starts to flood at the instant the regard becomes mutual, increases as the mutuality "threatens" to make the partners equal. It contains an inherent movement toward ecstatic participation. This is avoided by a return to the "real" world where relations may be objectified and managed. With an "As I was saying . . . ," we restore the conversation to its governable track. Sexism is the fear of equality, and fear of equality is dread of the holy infinite, which beats its wings around us ever more audibly as we give ourselves the more fully to those who are with us in the world.

The price to be paid for the liberated autonomy of women is high. Dissolution of many marriages, attacks upon tradition, bitter

controversies, sexual confusion, deep wounds to masculine preroga-
tive and ego, painful rites of learning to acknowledge one's oppression, and other dislocations of the social balance are parts of the
price already known. We may expect the price to go even higher
before we get a paradigm-shift in the culture which would allow the
conversation Marlo Thomas envisions to take place in a context of
social support. But even if society should change, the price of being
threatened by the infinite spirit of God with experiences of ecstasy
will remain. The holy, as I have said, is the "more" of any relation.
When any part of that "more" is domesticated, routinized, made
subject to religious doctrine, more appears, as beckoning and as
dreadful as what had come before.

A Christianity captive to Christ past will be increasingly forced to
draw lines of resistance to new forms of human encounter so as to
resist the emergent "more" of their spiritual and ethical field. Such
resistance is visible now in the alliance between Christian funda-
mentalism (Protestant, Catholic, and Mormon) and right-wing
politics, in which the opposition to feminism is key. Against this alliance, the churches that oppose it but nevertheless appeal to Christ
past as their authority are virtually powerless. If this continues, the
Christian church will lose not only its free women but also those
men, gradually increasing in number, who expect from women's
liberation a more authentic vision of their own destiny.

Many men are tired of upholding one half of a male/female
dichotomy in which we no longer truly believe, however much we
live in its habit. We look for a Christ to help us emerge, and we
wonder where she is. It is as if we had lost way back in infancy our
sister Christ, or as if we are awaiting her to be born.

·8·

Community and Christ

Life and relationship are synonymous. Everything that lives interacts with its environment, and even the individual organism, considered in itself, is a community of cells and organs, the whole giving meaning, form, and purpose to each of its members. "The eye cannot say to the hand, 'I have no need of you' " (I Cor. 12:21).

From the basic relatedness of life two moral principles emerge:

1. Denial of mutual need is denial of life itself and is therefore the self-defeating principle of evil. God cannot say to humanity, "I have no need of you." If God should say this, or if humanity says it, life is denied, turned against itself, twisted into a death-dealing form rightly named as evil.

2. Ethical decisions and values, insofar as they intend what is good, do not focus on *whether* people should be related but on the mode and quality of their interactions. Like life, goodness cannot occur in isolation. Good actions and values are those which contribute to a fructifying relatedness, while bad ones destroy it. Slavery, exploitation, and torture, although they are modes of relation, destroy their own basis by degrading and eventually killing the spirit of cooperation. The Nazis said to the Jews, "We need your forced labor for a time, but beyond that we have no need of you." Colonial planters in what is now Haiti exhausted their slaves quickly at hard labor and had to import a new slave population every twenty years. Sexism, racism, and anti-Semitism are morally wrong not sheerly because they treat some people as inferior, but because the underlying attitude is, "We do not need you to make us whole in

the same way that you need us." All discriminations in social status endanger the aim of life to become a community of mutual love and need.

To protect privilege was Jesus crucified. If we know anything about his death, we know that it was a political act performed by civil authorities. We may not know the ins and outs of the jockey-ings between the Roman governor, the local king, and the religious leaders, nor what role public opinion played; but we do know that to crucify was a mode of execution reserved to the Roman govern-ment and that Jesus was sentenced because his teachings were felt, no doubt correctly, as a threat to vested interests, both civil and religious. This threat surely arose from Jesus' expectation of a "kingdom" that would substitute the community of God for the known structures of civil and religious order. If this expectation died with him, it was resurrected with him, for Christianity was born in expectation of the overthrow of all structures of privilege in a "new age" to be created by God through the agency of Christ. Without some such expectancy, Christianity ceases to be Christian and has little to contribute to the world.

Christic expectation is in conflict not with all "human" values, as is sometimes said, but specifically with social structures which guarantee privilege at the expense of communal justice. This con-flict, dramatized in but not limited to the crucifixion of Jesus, together with christic expectation of an eventual community of God in the whole world, constitutes the Christian gospel. Neither the conflict nor the expectancy, however, are matters of information which a person may decide to believe or not. They are experiences. To speak of Christ and community is to discuss where and how a christic expectation and its conflict with society may be ex-perienced.

Contrary to most of the Reformed tradition in theology, I hold that the gospel is not communicated or made evident primarily in proclamation. We may preach *about* it, but we cannot preach *it*. The gospel, I maintain, is not a Word or a message, even if it is "good news." Rather, the gospel is a way of living which appears from time to time alongside what normally goes on in the social world. It is the occurrence of a kind of relatedness so compelling in its "promise" of things to come that it engenders expectation of a new age. The "promise" spoken of here is not a verbal pledge, not even a "sign" interpreted as an obligation of God that will be fulfilled later. Rather, it is the experience of community in awareness of the field of divine potential. It is the experience of the sacred power of life together.

One cannot understand gospel as an experience of things present and future so long as gospel is thought to be news of something that happened way back when. Insofar as Christ is Christ past, the gospel is merely a report, necessarily verbal, which has to be formulated and received in propositional form. Protestantism, with its great faith in scripture and preaching, is ever in danger of turning religion into mere theology, regarding theology as one's religion. The danger in Catholicism, meanwhile, is to suppose that in the Mass one re-experiences ever and again the one archetypal death and resurrection of Jesus. Both branches of Christianity have tried to subordinate gospel in present-future time to gospel as it once was, and for this reason they have a diminishing sense of religious expectancy. Expectancy is not born of information about something that has happened "in another country." Those events can at most shed light on what we know by firsthand experience.

Expectancy is a function of present action. I may hope for, or dread, certain things that I have heard of by report, but this does not cause me to *expect* them the way I have learned to expect my own death by observing how I am already in slow measure dying. The gospel is not so much a hearing as a tasting. That is why the Christian church is not primarily a school or an information center and is, above all, a community for the sharing of food. The reminder is especially important in an age of mass communication, when the churches may feel that their main task is to compete in the propaganda market of the media for access to people's minds. On the contrary, the task of the churches is to share food: that is, to perform those actions which generate christic expectation by way of experience of communal sharing. But this is frightening, because such experiences tend to become ecstatic.

We live in a cruel world, organized to protect and maintain social privilege, and no one can live in a community of christic expectation all the time. I must therefore speak of a community in its relation to the actual social world. To do so will require attention to religious ritual, but first I must make it clear that the social world in which we are living is hostile to all authentic forms of community.

The conditions of industrial life that have come about in the nineteenth and twentieth centuries, breeding impersonality, manipulation, and regimentation, corrode most efforts to sustain genuine communities. Intimate relationships such as families, friendships, and love affairs become ever harder to maintain. Institutions that are essentially communal such as churches, elementary schools, and theaters find that their communitarian bases in the society are more and more fragmented (cf. Driver 1970, pp. 455-469). Disruption of the ecosphere through pollution of air, land, and water is paralleled, and largely caused, by disruption of the "communosphere," by which I mean a human network of loyalty, accountability, and meaningful work in the world. We tend toward what Christopher Lasch, echoing Thomas Hobbes, has called "the war of all against all" (Lasch 1978, p. 26). Experience becomes privatized because its communal background is eaten away in repeated betrayals of human solidarity.

One hardly knows whether to say that the communosphere is the victim of rape, plunder, disease, decay, or demonic possession. That the rich are stealing from the poor, the powerful abusing the weak, is beyond question. What is open to doubt is the opinion that these injustices may be corrected by further manipulation of "the social system." It is clear that our problems are systemic, but it is not clear that the solutions lie in systems. The problem, if that is the right word for it, seems more and more to be the absence of a shared sense of human community as sacred. While Marxist societies attempt (and fail) to obliterate all thought of sacrality along with every practice of religion, the more capitalist societies pay lip service to the sacredness of individual human life without understanding that life is sacred only by virtue of its place in community.

What is holy is never an individual thing or person or even an individual God but rather the relation *between* one and another. The blasphemy of the German Holocaust, of Hiroshima, and of the Cambodian slaughter, to cite three of the clearest and most obscene examples, is not the sheer fact that so many people were murdered.

It is that their death was part of a campaign, which in Germany began long before the victims were gassed, to eject them from the human community. This intention, which so easily became a deed, had its worst effect not upon those who died but upon the human communities that survived. All of us who have lived through the time of these atrocities know that our sacred relations with one another have been violated, that we live in an age when the ties that bind us to our fellow creatures (*religio* means a uniting bond) can be severed with impunity. Our holy of holies has been desecrated. No priest and no God can protect our relations with one another now from being treated as garbage. The deepest insult is not to our individual dignities, bad as that may be, but to our loving. In a world in which nothing, not even loving, is sacred we find it difficult to resist internalizing the prevalent devaluation of our sacred bonds one to another. And as the resources of the planet become more scarce for sharing among ever more and more people, we inwardly prepare ourselves for a global *triage*: willingness to sacrifice *any* human relation for the sake of sheer survival. After all, if the *individual* is sacred, do we not have a sacred right to defend ourselves?

In *The Mountain People,* Colin Turnbull, an anthropologist, has described a small society of hunters and gatherers in East Africa who were deprived of their hunting grounds by governmental confiscation of their land. As severe hunger set in, all communal ties broke. Parents stole food from their children. Grown children stole from aged parents who could not forage for themselves and were left to die. Husbands and wives murdered each other. In a matter of months almost all trace of "human" behavior was gone (Turbull 1973). Here is a preview of what might occur in the later stages of that "war of all against all" in which the whole world is already participating. We see it in the behavior of nations toward each other and in the power plays of large corporations. It is also invading private life, and not only among the poor. Christopher Lasch is right to point out that the decimation of family life which has long been experienced by the inhabitants of slums is now being felt by the middle class, and for the same reason: "The collapse of personal life originates not in the spiritual torments of affluence but in the war of all against all, which is now spreading from the lower class, where it has long raged without interruption, to the rest of society" (Lasch 1978, p. 26).

We are witnessing today the not-so-gradual dissolution of the human network. Many rightly fear that the only thing to hold it together may be totalitarianism on an unprecedented scale (Heilbroner 1974). We know, however, that totalitarian order is not communal, for it is the imposition of system at the expense of freedom and love. The absence of a regard of community as a sacred potential has left us between the Scylla of totalitarian order and the Charybdis of an economic rapacity which goes by the name of "freedom." The very word "community," insofar as it retains deep meaning for us, is increasingly privatized. The public sphere is full of programs, systems, bureaucracies, institutions, media, and propaganda. The private sphere has tiny, wistful communities and precarious "primary relationships." The idea of a public community sounds anachronistic and hypocritically rhetorical. This puts the churches in a very odd position. They aspire to be public communities in an age which does not believe in any such thing and has almost no idea what it would mean to regard human community as sacred. Blasphemies against community have been in this age so blatant that we feel like fools to regard communal bonding as the holy of holies. Is it not now as passe as the gods of Olympus or superstitions about ghosts? The most urgent religious question of our time is also a social one: whether there exists in God, humanity, and the world a potential for the creation of genuine community, and if so, whether this potential is great enough to warrant an expectant faith in its power. It will not be sufficient, I think, to fall back on a mere "promise" of redemption once made in the biblical revelation, as does the so-called theology of hope (Moltmann 1967). That is to lodge one's faith in a power that is external, a matter of memory and hope bearing no relation to the evidence of present experience. What is vital is to know what needs to be done in order to bridge the passage between the promises once given and that community of peace which is not yet, in spite of all, a dream forgotten. The religious hunger of this age is expressed in the prayer "Show us the way." Its poignancy arises from the fact that we are now in a wilderness unlike any through which humanity has wandered before. The way through it is going to have to be improvised by us or by God or by both together.

To speak of Christ and community, then, is to speak of Christ the improvisor and of a community without a center, without clear boundaries, and with no secure place of dwelling. One must speak of a community not only willing to endure the pain of uncertainty but drawing its strength from the solidarity it creates in the face of events both hostile and unpredictable. This puts us in a position similar to that which may be imagined of people in the days when religions first began, having to improvise communal relations and to find ways of celebrating human, natural, and divine potential in a threatening and mysterious environment.

The Christian temptation, as I see it, is to suppose that we already know the way we should follow because it is already revealed in Christ. A similar temptation is to posit an ideal community *centered upon* the figure of Christ. By following "the way of Christ" and by participating in communion with him, Christians may suppose that they hold the key to the eventual solidarity of the human community. A christocentric community, however, does not answer to the need for creativity which the perils and the evils of this day place upon us. I suggest that we start with human community and then see what we are led to expect of Christ in present-future time. The traditional name for this motif is "advent." While it is true that the biblical Christ generated a new community, which came to be called Christian, it is also true that he came *to* an existing community, which was partly Jewish and partly a mixture of other traditions in the eclectic Hellenistic culture of that time. Christ did not then enter a vacuum but came into a pluralistic society already stirred up by a great variety of expectations.

I readily confess that I do not have the wisdom to propose a political solution for the social evils to which I have alluded. I do not believe anyone else has it either. As between capitalism and socialism I am a socialist, but I have no reason to think that any socialist party (or theory) of which I am aware knows how to overcome the alienation that is destroying the human network today. Religion alone has the power to do that.

The advantage of socialism is that it takes society as its point of

departure and its end-in-view. It also recognizes that society includes the productive work that people do, so there is no divorce between the ideal of the common good and the nitty-gritty of labor,
marketing, and other social service. To make such a split is characteristic of capitalism, but also of the bureaucratic systems that
operate in both capitalist and socialist countries. The ideology of
capitalism is to place individual initiative and private gain at the
apex of value, claiming that this in the long run is best for society.
Karl Marx saw through this rhetoric, which glosses over the exploitation of workers by those who reap profit from productive
systems. He proposed a plan of social ownership, which was all to
the good, but he did not solve the problem of management, which
remains to plague all societies that require large-scale organization.
Today, organization of supplies of raw materials, their transporta-
tion, use in manufacturing, and the distribution of goods produced
are global. The labor market is also global. That is why the possibility of human community is now a global concern, at which
point it reveals itself also as a spiritual matter. Socialism is correct
in regarding all human problems and solutions as social, not inherently private or individual. It is also right in seeing these problems
as inseparable from the way we do productive work. It is wrong
when it supposes that the solution to these problems can be found
apart from religious life.

The world today is confronted with the challenge of achieving a
just, religious, and open-ended organization of human work. At
present, our efforts at organization tend to stifle or freeze religious
expectancy. They also tend to emphasize control at the expense of
creative imagination. In this, they usually find the churches to be
their willing allies, for the churches are convinced that what we
need is conformity. They easily equate conformity to the Christ of
the past with conformity to what the managers of society demand.
Is there a way to keep organization, management, and religious life
radically open to the sacred quality of human community and its
potential? I think there may be, and that we should look for it, of
all places, in religious ritual.*

---

*My thinking about rituals is much indebted to Richard Schechner. I recommend
especially his *Essays on Performance Theory* (1977). Schechner in turn has been influenced

Some time ago, when I announced a course on rituals, numbers of people approached me with a single question: Why do rituals sometimes "work" and sometimes not? At first I tried to answer this question by analyzing the various components of ritual structures, thinking that if a ritual were adequately conceived and performed, then it would surely do whatever it was supposed to do. This line of inquiry did not yield very much, because the components of rituals are so varied that no "ideal" structure seems to emerge. Gradually another way of answering the question presented itself: rituals "work" when those who take part in them make clear demands upon the powers the ritual is designed to invoke.

A religious ritual is an encounter between visible and invisible participants. When the ritual itself becomes the object of attention, the encounter does not take place, or is diminished. When the focus is on the encounter, the visible participants make themselves intensely present, demanding the response of the invisible. What is meant by the ritual's "working" is the experience of intense presence, modified and interpreted according to the life context which has occasioned a particular ritual performance.

A similar concept is to be found in Schechner's viewing of all types of performance along a continuum between the poles he calls "efficacy" and "entertainment" (Schechner 1977, pp. 63-98). An aesthetic performance (in the commercial theater, let's say) is predominantly entertainment. Its main function is to provide pleasure through the artfulness of the performance. A religious ritual, meanwhile, is predominantly a matter of efficacy. Its principal function is to bring about or negotiate some change in the life situation of the community through a new encounter with invisible potencies.

What is of interest is the fact that efficacy and entertainment are inherently related, the one always mixed in some measure with the other. From the point of view of a rational empiricism, the efficacy of something would seem to have nothing to do with its entertainment value, while a "pure" aestheticism would not regard social efficacy as having any part in the realization of aesthetic pleasure.

by, and has come to exert a reciprocal influence upon, the anthropologist Victor Turner, whose theory about the meaning and function of rituals was first set out in *The Ritual Process* (1969) and has been further developed in subsequent publications.

The link between the two is revealed in what we know as "play," and this human activity provides the clue to the role religious rituals may "play" in the regeneration of community.

In the spontaneous playing that children do we are able to observe the most intense seriousness combined with an attitude of frivolity. On one level childplay is simply something to pass the time, an occupation of mind and body more pleasurable than empty hours or the doing of things required by grown-ups. On this level, the aim is merely to play, as one can notice from the fact that children often take a meandering path to hit upon the particular activity which promises the most pleasure. As the "game" gets going, however, it acquires a certain seriousness, wherein a second level of meaning appears. Concentration deepens. The game offers challenges that must be surmounted. Things can go wrong, leading to great frustration or else the re-doing of them so that they come out right. Child play usually includes much imitation of adult behavior, and it is well known that in play children acquire a large part of their learning. It is not difficult to see that in addition to its entertainment value play is efficacious. It accomplishes at least two kinds of beneficial result: the acquisition of skills and the experience of community among those who participate.

The relation of childplay to the "real" world of grown-ups is ambivalent or dialectical, and this is also true of adult play. The dialectic becomes most strong in religious rituals, which can be exceedingly ambivalent in their relation to the "secular" arrangements and duties of society. Victor Turner's contribution has been to see this ambivalence as belonging to a dialectic, which he calls "the ritual process."

Every society, Turner points out, is organized into social structures of one kind or another. The structures call, let us say, for certain types of leadership and specify who the leaders will be or at least how they are to be chosen. The structures regulate what work is to be done, by whom, when, and usually how. The structures govern marriage, divorce, childcare, all manner of family responsibilities as well as those connected with wage-earning, social services, taxation, warfare, and so on. In all this there may be greater or less freedom, but the freedom is circumscribed and given limits by the social structure, which is a combination of explicit rules or laws and implicit moral understandings. Even if a society were anarchistic (having no laws), it would require a structure of social mores in order to continue as a society. A society and its structure are virtually identical, and this is a reminder that language, too, is part of the social structure, its usage governed by rules that are partly explicit (to be learned at school) and partly just "understood" by everybody.

Victor Turner envisions rituals as standing "outside" the social structure. Although it is true that societies make room for rituals at certain times and places, even encouraging them with certain privileges (tax exemption and police protection, for example), it is also true that rituals sanction many kinds of behavior which are otherwise forbidden by the social structure. An extreme example is sexual orgy. Less extreme, far more widespread, are trance and spirit possession. More common still is ecstatic dancing and singing. Common to all rituals is a festive character, which may be high-spirited as in a black church at Easter or solemn as in a requiem mass. Every ritual is characterized by behavior that is special to it, different in some important way from the quotidian manners ordained by the social structure. As Margaret Mead once remarked, an anthropologist in a foreign country can tell when a ritual is about to occur "because the people walk different." At the least, in a ritual we expect special costumes, music, chants, recitations, and bodily movements.

Victor Turner's theory of "ritual process" may be clarified by comparison with earlier theories advanced by Emile Durkheim, Arnold van Gennep, and Mircea Eliade. I leave aside other important theories, notably the structuralism stemming from Claude Levi-Strauss, because I wish to keep my brief discussion focused on the communal aspect of religious ritual, its relation to society at large, and its effect upon social change. These have been Turner's concerns also. Durkheim, one of the founders of modern anthropology, provided a secular interpretation of religion, while Eliade's is a religious interpretation different in kind from Turner's. Gennep's theory provided the conceptual category, "liminality," which Turner proceeded to develop in his own way.

Durkheim (1915), basing his thought on the positivism of natural science, ruled out the possibility that the invisible powers addressed in religious ritual have any objective reality. He had therefore to

regard them as projections. Had he been a psychologist like Freud
or Jung, he might have seen the powers addressed in religious ritual
as projections of unconscious desires in the psyche. As he was interested, however, in a social theory, he envisioned them as projections
of certain aspects of society itself. He suggested that religious rituals
serve to consolidate and maintain the structures of social cohesion
by giving to them the appearance of divine sanction. The rituals reinforce social pressures by transforming them into sacred obligations. The masks, costumes, music, special words, and other ac-
coutrements of ritual are devices of projection whereby the social
good may be seen to be writ large in the heavens. Religion is society
santified.

Arnold van Gennep (1908), noticing that many rituals are "rites
of passage" from one social status to another, came to think that
transformation of status provides the *raison d'être* of all rituals.
Rites of name-giving, circumcision, initiation, marriage, childbirth, death, and so on serve to mark and protect the transitions,
always felt as dangerous or crisis-laden, between one stage of life
and another. Inaugurations, ordinations, crownings, etc., mark
passage from a former social status to a new one. Gennep's analysis
of such rituals showed that they are made up of three stages, one
corresponding to the old status, another corresponding to the new,
and (very important) an in-between stage, a kind of no-man's land,
which he called the "threshold" or (in Latin) the *limen*. All rituals
therefore include, he pointed out, a stage which is "liminal," repre-
senting an undefined or chaotic "nowhere" through which one must
pass on the way from the old to the new. This is the crisis stage,
during which the person is free of all social standing and has no
identity. It is a stage at once spiritual and threatening. The danger
of it makes ritual all the more necessary, while its mystery ensures
that the ritual shall be religious and not merely a kind of social
management. As I have noted, Gennep's concept of the "liminal" in
ritual was later adopted and put to further use by Victor Turner.

The scholar of comparative religions, Mircea Eliade, has viewed
rituals quite differently. In *Rites and Symbols of Initiation* (1958)
he proposed that rituals are reenactments of ideal ways of doing
things understood to have been established at the beginning of
time. These reenactments are necessary to counteract the effects of

historical change, which pull society away from its foundation in ideal patterns of behavior originally given by the gods. It follows that rituals have an essentially conservative purpose. They are intended to restore corrupted patterns of behavior and to relieve human beings of the burden of living always in historical time with its arduous labor and its terrifying decisions. In a ritual one can, for the moment, "get it right"; and "right" is the way it was in the very beginning, before time and error made things wrong. In Eliade's theory, emphasis falls upon the *form* of rituals and their putative correspondence to ideal forms of origin.

The theory of Victor Turner is far more dialectical than those of Durkheim, Gennep, and Eliade. Its philosophical roots appear to be Hegelian, not the positivism of Durkheim, the phenomenology of Gennep, or the Platonic idealism of Eliade. In any case, Turner conceives of rituals as having an antithetical relation to social structures in a dialectical process of change. For him, rituals are certainly not religion's way of projecting social sanctions onto the heavens, as they were for Durkheim. Neither are they ideal forms of behavior ordained by the gods, as in Eliade. He regards Gennep as having understood them better, although in a scheme that was too linear and thus too close to social necessity. Turner has therefore suggested that liminality is not merely one of the stages in a ritual but is the quality which defines the ritual as a whole. The entire ritual, conceived in relation to the structures and behaviors of everyday life, is liminal. With this insight, Turner is able to view rituals as "antistructures" over against the normal structures of daily life in society. A ritual, perhaps one could say, is an "alternative life-style" adopted for the ritual occasion. It enables people to dramatize and participate in a field of meaning not accessible under the rules of privilege, duty, and compromise that prevail in the social structure. As an occasional alternative to the social structure, religious ritual provides an antithesis to society's thesis and therefore induces a dialectical process of historical change. The inducement of change in society by way of its dialectical engagement with ritual is what Turner means by "the ritual process." Needless to say, the process gradually changes the rituals also.

To understand the process better, we must consider Turner's thoughts about human community as the basis both of social structure and of its antistructure in ritual. His suggestion is that societies are formed not only to enable the survival of their individual members but also to protect the existence of communitarian life. The aim of social life, we might say, is communal life, which is a value transcending material necessity and therefore is spiritual or religious. The trouble is that societies thwart their communal aim by the very means they adopt as necessary to make it possible. Social structures turn out not only to afford social cohesion but also to engender alienation.

The process of social alienation, familiar from the writings of Hegel and Marx, can occasionally be observed with great clarity, as I discovered during a brief visit to Papua New Guinea in 1976. There it was possible to see a society existing in two stages of development at once, the two as different as the neolithic and the jet age. The Enga people in the western highlands lived in almost total isolation until 1948, when an Australian patrol post was established in their territory. The culture was that of the late stone age, food provided mostly by gardens well cultivated on small-family homesteads. Hierarchal organization was minimal. In the councils of clan and tribe, the opinions of elder men were given deference, although a consensus of all adult men was required before action could be taken. Leadership in battle, trading, and ceremonials (all closely related one to another) was exercised by self-made entrepreneurs latterly known as "big men." Such leadership was more informal than formal, tended to last no more than about ten years, was not hereditary, and did not result in the accumulation of permanent wealth. The main hierarchical division in the society was sexual, since men held sway over women in every public way, the power of women over men confined to whatever persuasions and stratagems they might come up with informally, mostly at home. The indigenous Enga society, which has by no means disappeared, was characterized by a very clear sexual hierarchy and yet the virtual absence of class differentiation, inequality of wealth, or much division of labor. The men lived in intimate, egalitarian relation with each other. Because of the sexual hierarchy, the society's communitarian life was most fully realized among the men, who spent much time, including their sleeping hours, in the ceremonial "men's house." When I asked a young boy what the men did in their

house, he replied, "They eat, sleep, and tell stories. It's a good life."
I did not have to believe him entirely in order to see that the men's
house represented the communitarian ideal of the society. Women,
meanwhile, did not have a communal site. Each woman with children had her own house, where she took care of the children, the
pigs, the garden, and any unattached grown women who had no
better place to dwell.

With the Australians and other "Europeans" after 1948 the Enga
were introduced to money, cash crops, airplanes, roads, trucks,
hired labor, census registration, schools, churches, laws, and
eventually a democratic government based on the British parlia-
mentary system. A European social structure was thus laid down on
top of the indigenous one, and an outsider is able rather clearly to
see the alienations that the new structure has introduced as the ac-
companiment of the increased trade, travel, communication, education, and other unitive phenomena which it has also brought.
The society has become far more hierarchical than it was before,
and the sexual hierarchy, while it has been softened in a few ways
(for instance, by the schooling of girls alongside boys), has been reinforced in others (for instance, the education of boys in the English
language, which has become the legal language of the country,
while most of the girls are taught only pidgin English, the language
of the marketplace). As the men are the ones brought more fully
into the new social structure, they are the ones who show the most
alienation. Among its signs are alcoholism, unemployment,
thievery, and confusion about social roles. These are prices paid
worldwide for the increasing complexity of social structure in
modern societies. They appear in every land, most of all among
those groups which have to adapt suddenly to structures vastly different from those of their heritage, and especially when their mala-
daptation is profitable to other groups at or near the top of the
social structure.

Returning to Victor Turner's thesis, I take up his suggestion that
the alienation which accompanies social structure prevents society
from fulfilling a spiritual need which lies, ironically, in society's
very foundations. His name for this fundamental human need,
which may also be called an aspiration, is *communitas*. The Latin
term combines the idea of community with that of communion.

The thought is that people desire not only to live in community (already a deeper idea than that of a society) but to experience therein a sacred communion of life with life, something which the hierarchical structures of society inhibit and even condemn. The desire for *communitas* then expresses itself in religious rituals and is their principal *raison d'être*.

It is of course true that rituals display structures of their own. It is even true that their structures often imitate those of the society, replicating it symbolically. Turner proposes, however, that ritual structure is to social as antithesis is to thesis. Although it may (or may not) resemble the social structure, it is *not* the social structure. By its very artifice it reveals the artificial in the otherwise compelling social structure. The ritual is a temporary, more or less ideal, alternative structure thrown up beside the regnant social structure. Being a form of play, it is an antistructure. While it acknowledges the social structure, it finds ways to distance, judge, abrogate, and even mock it. The major evidence for this is that rituals tend toward ecstatic transport in which communion with the god, with nature, and with other communicants provides an occasion for overcoming the structured differences that customarily obtain. A time out of time, a structure out of structure, religious ritual aspires to a *communitas* more fully social than society. The sacred is the communitarian.

Turner's thesis would lead us to expect a positive correlation between the more communitarian forms of worship and the more alienated segments of society, and I believe this could be shown to be the case by and large. Within Christianity, liturgical hierarchy became pronounced when this religion was adopted by Roman and Byzantine emperors. Ecstatic forms of Christian worship are regularly condemned by churches that have a strong investment in the social structure. They grow up from time to time nonetheless, almost always among the dispossessed, as, for instance, in Pentecostalism. In regions of vast poverty such as Latin America, the liturgical hierarchical structure of the official Catholic religion becomes mixed with ecstatic ritual practices retained from African and native American religions. These phenomena may be seen to indicate that religion is escapist, as Marx taught, or that it aims at the transformation of society in the direction of *communitas*. Although it is clear to me that religion, certainly the Christian religion, is often escapist, I agree with Turner in thinking that mere compensation for social inequity is neither its principal purpose nor its usual function. I would cite as evidence the pains that social rulers take either to destroy religions or to bring them in line. I think also, even if I am not in position to prove it, that rituals become the more escapist as they become the more hierarchically structured, for then it is easiest, if I may so put it, to treat them as "spectator sports." The danger religion poses to the status quo of a social structure is to enable people to experience, not only to hear about, communal equality.

The license of rituals, in some ways analogous to that of theater, has numerous effects upon society. It prevents, as I have suggested, the social structure's being taken as absolute or final. The presence of antistructure alongside structure introduces, or at least drama-tizes, an instability within society, allowing the need for *com-munitas* to be expressed and the occasional experience of *com-munitas* to exert pressure upon social arrangements in the direction of equality and freedom of exchange. Occasionally religious rituals become the breeding-ground for direct social action or revolution, as in the slave rebellion in Haiti in 1791–1800, the civil rights move-ment led by Martin Luther King in the 1960's, or the overthrow of the Shah of Iran in 1979. These examples, incidentally, show that ritual antistructure does not in itself provide an adequate basis for the organization of society. It gives voice, shape, and transitory experience to an aspiration and is therefore a moral disturber of the society but does not by itself produce good government. This does not mean, however, as post-Enlightment thinking has often con-cluded, that religious rituals are irrelevant to the pursuit of social justice. Indeed, says Victor Turner (1977, p. 39),

> Growing evidence convinces me, that new ways of modeling or fram-ing social reality may actually be proposed and sometimes legiti-mated in the very heat of performance, emerging as a sort of artifact of popular creativeness. That is why public liminality has often been regarded as "dangerous" by whatever powers-that-be who represent and preside over established structure. Public liminality can never be tranquilly regarded as a safety valve, mere catharsis, "letting off

steam," rather it is *communitas* weighing structure, sometimes finding it wanting, and proposing in however extravagant a form new paradigms and models which invert or subvert the old.

The failure of much ritual life to have a liberating or egalitarian effect upon society does not lie in the nature of rituals themselves, contrary to what many people believe and what the theories of Durkheim and Eliade both suggest. The conservative or reactionary function of religious rituals is due to their co-optation by social leaders, who often include, to be sure, the priests themselves. I. M. Lewis, in his scholarly study of *Ecstatic Religion* (1971), has drawn a useful distinction between "peripheral" and "central" religious cults. The latter worship spirits regarded as central to the social and natural orders, while the former invoke spirits from outside, spirits who are tangential to the social order and in some cases directly opposed to it. Lewis emphasizes that members of the peripheral cults tend to come from those parts of the population who are downtrodden, outcast, or in some other way socially inferior. I suggest that peripheral cults have repeatedly become central by processes of co-optation, which can employ two strategies.

A first co-optive strategy is to manipulate the ritual's occurrence in such way that the communitarian impulses are simply released, as if the ritual were indeed an escape valve. To do this, the ritual's component of efficacy (in Schechner's phrasing) is downplayed while its entertainment value is magnified. People may be taught not to expect that the ritual will have any effect except perhaps on one's emotions or one's "private" life. In this work of co-optation theologians and other theorists often assist by offering "structuralist" interpretations of liturgy which reduce it to a set of symbols arranged in coherent form. The ritual then becomes intellectually or aesthetically or emotionally satisfying, perhaps even cathartic, but without any expected impact on the social world.

A second strategy of co-optation is to bring the ritual as far as possible into conformity with the social structure, which it will then seem merely to enhance. The first step in this strategy is to make sure that the leaders of ritual are given an honored place within society and encouraged to wear their ceremonial garb on all social occasions so that people come to identify the power of the priest, minister, or shaman with that of the state. The second step is to routinize everything in the religious rituals that is uncanny, ecstatic, or magical. As Max Weber (1968) spoke of the ability of institutions to routinize charisma, accommodating prophetic voices to the routines of society, so we may think of a routinization of rituals to the same end. So successful has this often been that many people think of rituals as inherently routine, nothing more than the endless repetition of prescribed words and gestures. The sad fate of rituals in many societies is to lend themselves to ritualism, as if the form of the ritual guaranteed something in itself.

Theodore Jennings (1978) has pointed out that rituals are characterized not only by relative stability of their forms over long periods of time but also by innovations made as they are performed. Such innovations are familiar to students of the history of liturgy. Sometimes changes in rituals can be traced to important events or new conditions in society, but Jennings stresses, as does Turner above, the role played by improvisation within the *performance* of the ritual. This he compares with improvisations made when one is dancing, singing, or making any kind of art, and his point is that the improvisatory moments are occasions of discovery and learning. The ritual performer acts himself or herself into new territory, so to speak. The community of ritual participants finds itself engaged in something not done just this way before and acquires thereby an altered sense of its life in the world. Alongside the fact that rituals are repeated over and over we need to recognize that this very repetition provides occasion for creativity, just as it does in music and dance. The purpose of such repetition is not merely to keep things steady. It is also to provide a medium and a springboard for transformation. What gets changed is not only the worshipper but also the ritual form, and the history of religions indicates that the gods change, too. As there is a dynamism in the prophetic voices of religion which call for justice and charity transcending what society has settled for, so there is also a dynamism in religion's priestly and ritual life. At its best it constitutes a critique of the social structures through experiences of deep communication and liberated expectancy. This is the context for understanding the community of Christ.

Teachings about the relation of Christ to the human community are derived from liturgical practice. In patterns of worship, which include preaching and the use made of scripture as parts of the total ritual setting, the person of Christ is formed, for better or worse. This perhaps frightening fact leads to a sobering christological insight: Christ is Christ only within the *communitas* of worship. It follows that the relation of Christ to human society is dependent upon what transpires in the *koinonia* (communal life) of Christians. The Christian contribution to love, peace, justice, and creativity in the world cannot be greater than the actual presence of these qualities in the *koinonia* of christic expectation. Here is one reason for the perniciousness of doctrines of the perfection of Christ. They lead the church to dream (or even to boast) of its own perfection, being drawn then either to triumphalism or to a sectarian piety. Lost is the recognition that Christ, whether past, present, or future, is only one part of the divine life. It is the part which operates through the eucharistic meal.

The assertion that Christ is Christ only within the *communitas* of worship stands in opposition to the thought that Christ is a personage with status in the social structure. I shall remind us later of the dialectic between ritual and society, but the first step is to relinquish all claims concerning a status of Christ in the sociopolitical world. We are not concerned with a singular Christ who came "once for all" and whose claims are therefore universal, essentially the same for the church and the world and for all times and places. We are concerned with many Christs. There are many because Christ is the human form of actual encounters between God and the world. As life changes, the encounters change, and it is a matter of plain history that Christ is envisioned in vastly different ways by differing groups of Christians. This being the case, the attempt to claim an objective social status for Christ is nothing other than a projection onto society of Christians' own claims to status. Like all projections, it serves to bypass the moral responsibility of the ones who make the projection. A more responsible path is to understand Christ as a presence within the ritual community and then to determine what value that *community* has and may have for the society at large.

Most Christian sermons and pronouncements by church bodies

on social matters imply that Christ is the foundation of the whole world, whose recognition as such by the churches entitles them to speak. The assumption that Christ is "Lord of all" entails the idea that Christ is a personage of the highest social status and that if "every knee should bow" to him, all would be well. Even if this assumption is tempered by awareness that the reign of Christ is an eschatological vision, and even if it is understood as the paradox of a "king" who is in fact a "suffering servant," it still maintains the principle of Christ's eventual triumph in society. The worship of Christ in ritual thus becomes not only a projection but also a kind of secret or mysterious knowledge which the whole earth would share if only its mind were not darkened. I mentioned that the churches tend either toward triumphalism or sectarian piety. I may add that the triumphalism, which arises from christic projection, is in psychological terms a megalomania and in political terms a fascism. Sectarian piety, being the flip side of the same perfectionism, is sanctified loneliness, deeply hostile to the *risks* involved in all communitarian life.

The swing of the churches' imagination between triumphalism and lonely marginality is the result of not grasping, or perhaps not loving, the dialectical difference and interplay between social structure and ritual antistructure. If it is constricting to say that Christ belongs only to the eucharistic community, I must point out that it is also liberating. When it is grasped that Christ belongs to the playfulness of Christian ritual, then the heart can be given fully to the expectation of Christ. Nothing is more wholehearted than play. Conversely, to ensconce Christ as a social personage who either is or ought to be acknowledged by everyone is to introduce a pretension into the social structure, compounding the claims to privilege already operative there. The result is "bad faith." Long aware of this, theologians have warned against ignoring the difference between the church and the world. However, they have at the same time often suggested that the church is higher and more close to the truth than is the social world.

I am suggesting that truth arises from the difference and the interaction between the church and the world. When this difference is blurred, the interaction is weakened. The condition is one known to Gestalt psychology as "confluence." Lines of demarcation and separate identity go unrecognized in the aim to swallow up or be swallowed by the "other." Confluence impairs communication. The church can address the world and bear witness to the world only when it recognizes the world as a legitimate "you." Pretensions to Christian discipleship on the part of political powers can then be unmasked, while the social necessity of exercising power within the limits of justice can be affirmed. I suppose that when Jesus said render to Caesar what is Caesar's and to God what is God's (Mark 12:17), he did not enunciate a policy of "peaceful coexistence." He pointed, I suppose, to two kinds of structure which have meaning for each other by virtue of their difference. Christ can be Christ only within the spaces of Christian ritual.

Even there, however, one has to be careful. Within the eucharistic ritual, as long as it is a genuine antistructure, Christ does not function as center, model, or norm but plays another role of a far more open character.

Christ gravitates to the center-point of sacramental practice when the antistructure of liturgy apes the structures of society too much and too long. An increasing centrality of Christ has marked the routinization of Christian ritual. By social inertia within the church, its ritual comes to repeat itself steadily, acquiring a character of "perfection" analogous to that of its centralized Christ. A social hierarchy grows up within the church, maintaining rights of sacramental leadership. Stability and continuity come to seem more important than the transports of *communitas*. Improvisation is discouraged. Even Spirit is routinized.

If it is remembered that experiences of *communitas* are the soul of ritual, it can be seen that at its best a ritual does not have a fixed center. The rituals of non-European peoples often seem chaotic or unfocused to Western eyes, which have grown accustomed to the centrality of altar, Bible, priest, or some other representation of "Christ the center." At *vaudoux* ceremonies in Haiti I had trouble keeping track of the *mambo* (priestess) because she moved all over the place, very seldom making herself the point of focus. Although the *vaudoux* ceremony does actually circle around a center-pole, said to be a kind of sacred tree or *axis mundi*, this is not where the action occurs. The main event is the entry of one divine spirit or another into this or that worshipper, and this occurs wheresoever it pleases on the dance-floor. Similarly, the big Tee ceremonial I photographed in Enga territory in New Guinea appeared so chaotic that I had great difficulty learning how it was put together. These examples do not suggest lack of structure but rather a kind of structure which creates what Richard Schechner has called an "open grid," any part of which may become the locus of an unforeseen encounter. More important than center, even if there is one, is the ambient dynamic field.

Christian ritual also deemphasizes symbolic centers when it rises out of its routine to approach *communitas*. At such times neither Christ nor God nor Spirit nor any representative of them is central. To the extent that a Christian community focuses upon a central figure, even if that be God or Christ, it is not a *communitas* but a social hierarchy. Theologically speaking, it is monistic rather than trinitarian. In psychological terms, it is introverted. From an ethical point of view, it has ceased to find religious value in relations of mutual parity.

If Christ is not sought at the center of Christian ritual, then where? To answer briefly, I reply with a scriptural phrase: "in the breaking of bread" (Luke 24:35). Departing from the image of a center, I reach for another and am driven, like Luke, to parable.

In the breaking of bread is expectation. If I move beyond the routine of sharing food with those at table, if I bring myself to the act fully present, ready to divide the food and share it with those who are next to me, if I admit that I have never shared this same food before, have never been at this same juncture of time and space and will return here no more, if I am ready to let the sharing be what it will be, my heart leaps. I may not know what to expect, but I am expectant. Time stops the way a dancer's leap pauses at the apex of its arc. To stay there would be absurd. Not to come there at all is the pathos of routine. But I am here, face to face with others on the brink of sharing. In that pause of expectancy is Christ, Emmanuel, God with us.

One may say, "But this Christ has no face! *Whom* are you talking about?" I am not sure that this Christ has no face. It would be better to say this Christ has a thousand faces. And is that not the case? Is it not true that the Christ whose presence is anticipated in Christian worship is as variable as the needs of those who seek? Although in the moment of expectancy I do not know what to expect, my expectation is delineated by whatever need and whatever bliss I know in my life. It is further touched by what I discern of my neighbor's need. But what will happen now I do not know. The face of Christ as I yield myself to the breaking of the bread may surprise me. I have to be ready for one who comes *now*, in present-future time. It would be well if Christian worship included a time before people go home when they tell what Christ they have met as they broke the bread and gave it to each other. That would mean to break the bread a second time in exposures of the heart. It would mean to fulfill the act of worship not in private consumption of the offered sacrament but in a *communitas* of shared need and shared reward. It would mean the shattering of the one face of Christ into a thousand faces and the naked awareness that the unity of Christ is love in the presence of diversity.

Complete in itself, Christian worship is not complete in relation to society. On the contrary, it is the opening of a wound. The greater the experience of *communitas* in worship, the more painful its violations in the world at large. This pain, and not an abstract ideal of justice, is what motivates a Christian social ethic. When we leave the space of ritual and walk once more in the midst of the violence by which society maintains itself, we perceive that Christian worship is not the beginning, middle, or end of anything. It is one side of a dialectic, at its best a creative tension, which generates conscience. In Chapter 2, I spoke of conscience as the distinctive trait of human beings. The locus of conscience is not the individual but the community, where it arises to deal with conflict between competing interests and values. Ritual participation alone does not generate conscience. Neither does the social structure, which, left to itself, suppresses conscience for the sake of expediency. Conscience is needed, born, and educated in the gap between religious community and secular society.

Once more, we are drawn to the crucial importance of things that occur "in between." The ethical dynamic of life, like experience in general, occurs at points of boundary, places of threshold, moments of encounter and dangerous crossing. Spiritual and ethical life are always liminal. As *communitas* is liminal to society, so ethical decisions are liminal to them both.

At every threshold, the spiritual expresses itself as an expectancy. What will come, we ask, of this leap, this crossing? A Christian community, looking at the society from which it has momentarily withdrawn itself and to which it will return, needs ask, "What do we expect in this crossing?"

I write these words because I am disillusioned with the messages I hear from a self-assured Christianity. They declare that the truth is Christ as known in the church and therefore the task of Christians is to "apply" the truth to the world outside. Another version has it that this truth *cannot* be applied, so let the world go its way until the just shall be redeemed at the end of time. Lost from both stances is awareness that life happens in the act of relating.

Were the church to take itself more seriously, it would indulge itself more openly in the free play of christic expectation. Liberated from its certainty about Christ past, set free to improvise in its relation to Christ future, it could return to the threshold of society open to the creative possibilities of God. Christ is not a tree of knowledge, to taste whereof is to gain the knowledge of good and evil. To bring Christ to the world is not the end we should have in view. Instead, we should allow a present-future Christ to come to us in the breaking of bread. The communal body thus formed is in position to address the world — not in "truth" but in holy expectation.

Reference List

Arendt, Hannah
    1958   *The Human Condition*. Chicago: University of Chicago Press.

Augustine
                De Trinitate (The Trinity), in *Augustine: Later Works*, trans. John Burnaby. London: SCM Press Ltd., 1955.

Barstow, Anne
    1979   *The Defense of Clerical Marriage in the Eleventh and Early Twelfth Centuries: The Norman Anonymous and His Contemporaries*. Ph.D. dissertation, Columbia University.

Barth, Karl
    1936–1969   *Church Dogmatics*, ed. G. W. Bromiley and T. F. Torrance. Edinburgh: T. & T. Clark.

Berger, Peter L., and Luckmann, Thomas
    1966   *The Social Construction of Reality*. New York: Doubleday, Anchor Books, 1967.

Bettenson, Henry
    1947   *Documents of the Christian Church*. New York: Oxford University Press.

Bonhoeffer, Dietrich
    1967   *Letters and Papers from Prison*, revised edition, ed. Eberhard Bethge. New York: Macmillan.

171

Boswell, John
    1980   *Christianity, Social Tolerance, and Homosexuality.* Chicago: University of Chicago Press.

Buber, Martin
    1923   *I and Thou (Ich und Du)*, trans. Walter Kaufmann. New York: Charles Scribner's Sons, 1970.

The Catholic Theological Society of America
    1977   *Human Sexuality: New Directions in American Catholic Thought.* New York: Paulist Press.

Cobb, John B., Jr.
    1975   *Christ in a Pluralistic Age.* Philadelphia: The Westminster Press.

Cone, James H.
    1969   *Black Theology and Black Power.* New York: Seabury Press.

Cullmann, Oscar
    1950   *Christ and Time*, trans. Floyd V. Filson. Philadelphia: The Westminster Press.

Daly, Mary
    1978   *Gyn/Ecology: The Metaethics of Radical Feminism.* Boston: Beacon Press.

Driver, Tom F.
    1963   "On Taking Sex Seriously," in *Christianity and Crisis*, vol. 23 (October 14).

    1965   "Sexuality and Jesus," in *Union Seminary Quarterly Review*, XX.3 (March 1965), pp. 235-246.

    1970   *Romantic Quest and Modern Query: A History of the Modern Theater.* New York: Delacorte. Reprinted at Washington, D.C.: University Press of America, 1980.

    1977   *Patterns of Grace: Human Experience as Word of God.* San Francisco: Harper & Row.

Durkheim, Emile
    1915   *The Elementary Forms of Religious Life*, trans. J. W. Swain. London: Allen & Unwin. Paperback edition, New York: Free Press, 1965.

Einstein, Albert
1950   *The Meaning of Relativity*. Princeton: Princeton
                             University Press.

Eliade, Mircea
1958   *Rites and Symbols of Initiation*. New York: Harper
                             Colophon.

Fiorenza, Elizabeth
1978   "Women in the Pre-Pauline and Pauline Churches,"
                             in *Union Seminary Quarterly Review*, vol. 33, nos. 3
                             & 4 (Spring & Summer 1978), pp. 153-166.

Foucault, Michel
1978   *The History of Sexuality*, vol. I, trans. Robert Hurley.
                             New York: Pantheon Books.

Frazer, James George, Sir
1890   *The Golden Bough*. Ed. and abridged by Theodor H.
                             Gaster. New York: S. G. Phillips, 1959.

Frye, Northrop
1957   *Anatomy of Criticism*. Princeton: Princeton
                             University Press.

Geertz, Clifford
1965   "The impact of the concept of culture on the concept
                             of man," in *New Views of Man*, ed. John R. Platt,
                             Chicago: University of Chicago Press.

Gennep, Arnold van
1908   *The Rites of Passage*, trans. Monika B. Vizedom and
                             Gabrielle E. Caffee. Chicago: University of Chicago
                             Press, 1960.

Gilkey, Langdon
1976   *Reaping the Whirlwind: A Christian Interpretation
                             of History*. New York: Seabury Press.

Harris, Marvin
1974   *Cows, Pigs, Wars, and Witches*. New York: Random
                             House.

Harvey, Van
1966   *The Historian and the Believer*. New York: The
                             Macmillan Company.

Heilbroner, Robert L.
1974   *An Inquiry into the Human Prospect*. New York: Norton.

Homans, Peter
1979   *Jung in Context: Modernity and the Making of a Psychology*. Chicago: University of Chicago Press.

Infeld, Leopold
1950   *Albert Einstein: His Work and Its Influence on Our World*, revised edition. New York: Charles Scribner's Sons.

James, William
1902   *Varieties of Religious Experience*. New York: Longmans, Green, and Company.

Jarvie, I. C.
1964   *The Revolution in Anthropology*. London: Routledge & Kegan Paul. Chicago: Henry Regnery (Gateway Edition), 1969.

Jennings, Theodore
1978   "On Ritual Knowledge," a paper presented for the Ritual Studies Consultation of the American Academy of Religion.

Kee, Howard Clark
1977   *Community of the New Age: Studies in Mark's Gospel*. Philadelphia: The Westminster Press.

Koenig, John T.
1979   *Jews and Christians in Dialogue: New Testament Foundations*. Philadelphia: The Westminster Press.

Küng, Hans
1976   *On Being a Christian*, trans. Edward Quinn. New York: Doubleday and Co.

Kuhn, Thomas S.
1962   *The Structure of Scientific Revolutions*. Chicago: University of Chicago.

Lasch, Christopher
1978   *The Culture of Narcissism: American Life in an Age of Diminishing Expectations*. New York: Norton.

Lewis, I. M.
1971   *Ecstatic Religion: An Anthropological Study of Spirit Possession and Shamanism.* Baltimore: Penguin Books.

Lindsell, Harold
1976   *The Battle for the Bible.* Grand Rapids: Zondervan Publishing House.

Mead, Margaret
1970   *Culture and Commitment.* Garden City: Natural History Press (Doubleday & Co.).

Moltmann, Jürgen
1967   *Theology of Hope: On the Ground and the Implications of a Christian Eschatology.* New York: Harper & Row.

1974   *The Crucified God,* trans. R. A. Wilson and John Bowden. New York: Harper & Row.

Nelson, James B.
1977   "Homosexuality and the Church," in *Christianity and Crisis*, vol. 37, no. 5 (April 4), pp. 63–69.

1978   *Embodiment: An Approach to Sexuality and Christian Theology.* Minneapolis: Augsburg Publishing House.

Niebuhr, H. Richard
1943   *Radical Monotheism and Western Culture.* London: Faber and Faber.

Niebuhr, Richard R.
1972   *Experiential Religion.* New York: Harper & Row.

Nineham, Dennis
1976   *The Use and Abuse of the Bible: A Study of the Bible in an Age of Rapid Cultural Change.* London: The Macmillan Press Ltd.

Phipps, William
1970   *Was Jesus Married?* New York: Harper & Row.

1973   *The Sexuality of Jesus.* New York: Harper & Row.

Pirsig, Robert M.
1975   *Zen and the Art of Motorcycle Maintenance*. New York: Bantam Books.

Princeton Religion Research Center
1979   *Religion in America 1979–80*. Princeton, N.J.

Robinson, Edward
1977.   *The Original Vision: A Study of the Religious Experience of Childhood*. Oxford: The Religious Experience Research Unit.

Robinson, James M.
1959   *A New Quest of the Historical Jesus*. Naperville, Ill.: A. R. Allenson. London: SCM Press, 1970.

Robinson, John A. T.
1973   *The Human Face of God*. Philadelphia: Westminster Press.

Ruether, Rosemary Radford
1974   *Faith and Fratricide*. New York: Seabury Press.

Sanders, James A.
1975   Review of *Finding the Old Testament in the New*, by Henry M. Shires. *Union Seminary Quarterly Review*, XXX.2-4 (Winter-Summer 1975), pp. 245f.

Sartre, Jean-Paul
1948   *The Psychology of Imagination*, trans. of *L'Imaginarie: Psychologie phenomenologique de l'imagination*. New York: Philosophical Library.

1962   *Imagination: A Psychological Critique*, trans. Forrest Williams. Ann Arbor: University of Michigan Press.

Schechner, Richard
1977   *Essays on Performance Theory*. New York: Drama Books.

Schelling, Friedrich Wilhelm
1942   *The Ages of the World*, trans. Frederick de Wolfe Bolman, Jr. New York: Columbia University Press.

Schweitzer, Albert
1906   *The Quest of the Historical Jesus*, trans. W. Montgomery; second English edition, London: A. & C. Black, 1911.

Scott, Ernest Findlay
1932   *The Literature of the New Testament.* New York: Columbia University Press.

Slater, Philip E.
1970   *The Pursuit of Loneliness: American Culture at the Breaking Point.* Boston: Beacon Press.

Sobrino, Jon
1976   *Christology at the Crossroads.* Maryknoll, N.Y.: Orbis Books.

Sölle, Dorothee
1970   *Beyond Mere Obedience: Reflections on a Christian Ethic for the Future,* trans. Lawrence W. Denef. Minneapolis: Augsburg Publishing House.

1975   *Suffering.* Philadelphia: Fortress Press.

Tillich, Paul
1948   *The Protestant Era,* trans. James Luther Adams. Chicago: University of Chicago Press.

1951   *Systematic Theology,* Volume I. Chicago: University of Chicago Press.

1957   *Systematic Theology,* Volume II. Chicago: University of Chicago Press.

1963   *Systematic Theology,* Volume III. Chicago: University of Chicago Press.

Tracy, David
1975   *Blessed Rage for Order: The New Pluralism in Theology.* New York: Seabury Press.

Turnbull, Colin M.
1973   *The Mountain People.* New York: Simon and Schuster.

Turner, Victor
1969   *The Ritual Process: Structure and Anti-Structure.* Hammondsworth: Penguin Books.

1977   "Frame, Flow and Reflection: Ritual and Drama as Public Liminality," in *Performance in Postmodern Culture,* ed. Michel Benamou and Charles Caramello. Madison, Wis.: Coda Press.

Washbourn, Penelope G.
1972   "Differentiation and Difference—Reflections on the
                Ethical Implications of Women's Liberation," in
                Women and Religion: 1972, ed. Judith Plaskow
                Goldenberg. Missoula, Mont.: American Academy of
                Religion.

Weber, Max
1968   *On Charisma and Institution Building*. Selected
                papers, ed. S. N. Eisenstadt. Chicago: University of
                Chicago Press.

Whitehead, Alfred North
1929   *Process and Reality*. New York: Harper Torchbook
                edition, 1960.

Index

179

Christological concepts, 25
Christological formulations, 14, 25
Christological method, 8, 12
Christological norms, 28
Christological tradition, 29
Christology, 3, 5, 12, 29, 36, 49, 74; and
    doctrine of non-persons, 20; and ethics,
    x, 4, 21, 22, 23, 24; high and low, 19;
    and Judaism, 36
Church, 2, 11, 18, 47, 48, 51, 76, 77, 111,
    126, 140, 145, 151, 165-167, 170; as
    body of Christ, 40; and canon, 88, 89;
    and community, 148; and conscience,
    90; and ethics, 21; as New Israel, 58; as
    political, 91; and scripture, 90; and sex,
    128; as social base of theology, 12;
    sociology of, 89
Cobb, John, 43
Communitas, 56, 119, 120, 160-163, 167-
    169; and Christ, 165
Community, 31, 146, 150, 158, 160, 169,
    170; and Christ, 152, 164; of christic ex-
    pectation, 134; and church, 148; com-
    munal justice, 147; communal life, 129,
    159; communal relations, 152; and
    communion, 160, 161; communitarian
    impulse, 163; community of God, 147;
    communosphere, 149; experience of as
    promise, 148; and liturgy, 165; and
    play, 155; as privatized, 151; and ritual,
    156, 164; sexual community, 134, 137;
    Spiritual Community, 138
Cone, James, 113
Conscience, 21-23, 52, 55, 76, 84-86, 89,
    130. 169; and Christ, 24; and church,
    90; ethical conscience, 45; and love, 24
Context, 108, 110, 112, 138;
God as infinite context, 107; and Spirit,
    105, 111
Copernicus, 68, 69
Creativity of God, 64
Cullmann, Oscar, 43, 51
Cultural matrices, 73

Daly, Mary, 113
Darwin, Charles, 62, 71, 93
Dawson, Christopher, 18
Death, finality of, 17, 18
Divorce, 127; and marriage, 125, 131
Dogma, 1, 2
Donne, John, 69
Dualism, 50, 98, 100, 112, 113, 115, 122-
    124; conceptual, 112; cosmic, 134-136,
    138; dualistic ethics, 112; dualistic
    thinking, 124; monistic, 124, 134, 137;

public and private as, 139; relative, 134;
    sexual, 133, 134, 138
Durkheim, Emile, 156, 158
Dyad, 102

Efficacy and entertainment, 154, 163
Eliade, Mircea, 156, 157, 158
Einstein, Albert, 62, 68, 70, 71, 93
Eliot, T.S., 18, 43
Enlightment, the, 2, 6
Envisionment, 60
Eschatology, 30, 54, 60; eschatological
    context of New Testament, 49; escha-
    tological expectation, 50, 75, 120;
    eschatological vision, 35, 166; and the
    New Testament, 118
Eschaton, 40, 48, 51
Ethics, 22, 25, 55, 79, 83, 113; and Christ,
    47, 83; Christian social ethic, 169; chris-
    tological, 53; and christology, x, 21, 22,
    23, 24; communitarian, 31; and con-
    science, 45; and church, 21; dualistic,
    112; ethical expectation and, 46, 75;
    ethical fields, 145; ethical relativity,
    135; and experience, 16; and Jesus, 21,
    54; and sex, 122; sexual ethics, 124,
    132, 133; and theology, 13; and trini-
    tarian thinking, 97, 111, 112, 113
Evil, 146
Existential decision, 93
Expectation, 15, 86, 113-115, 143, 148,
    168, 169; christic, 134, 147, 165, 170;
    eschatological expectation, 50, 75, 120;
    ethical, 46, 75; messianic, 29, 32; reli-
    gious, 144
Experience, x, 4, 19, 26, 29, 54, 83, 94,
    147; privatized, 149; religious and
    ethical value of, 16; sexual, 121, 130;
    social, 130

faith, 6, 29, 77, 78, 115, 118; 'bad faith',
    166; and historical method, 8; and in-
    terest 111; and liberation, 29; and res-
    urrection, 7, 11
Faraday, Michael, 70
Female autonomy, 143
Feminism, 139, 141
Fields, and field theory, 70, 110; contex-
    tual fields, 104, 105; ecological fields,
    72; ethical fields, 145; dynamic fields,
    71, 168; infinite field of God's spirit,
    136; radiational fields, 135; relational
    fields, 75, 103, 144; spiritual fields, 137,
    145

181